Airborne

THE MORNINGSIDE DRAMAS
AIRBORNE

EDITED BY
ANN JANSEN

Blizzard Publishing • Winnipeg

Airborne: Radio Plays by Women first published 1991 by
Blizzard Publishing Ltd.
301–89 Princess St., Winnipeg, Canada R3B 1K6
© 1991 Ann Jansen

Cover art by Scott Barham
Cover design by Terry Gallagher
Printed in Canada by Hignell Printing Ltd.

Printed with the assistance of
the Canada Council and the Manitoba Arts Council.

The publishers wish to express their gratitude to Anna
Synenko for her help in preparing this publication.

Caution

This anthology is fully protected under the copyright laws of Canada
and all other countries of the Copyright Union and is subject to
royalty. Copyright for all material contained in this anthology is
retained by the authors individually. Rights to produce, in whole or
part, by any group amateur or professional, are retained by the
authors.
    No part of this book (including cover design) may be reproduced
or transmitted in any form, by any means, electronic or mechanical,
including photocopying, recording, and information storage and
retrieval systems, without permission in writing from the publisher,
except by a reviewer, who may quote brief passages in a review.

Canadian Cataloguing in Publication Data
Main entry under title:

Airborne: radio plays by women
    Anthology of plays originally broadcast on CBC's Morningside
program.
    ISBN 0-921368-22-4

1. Radio plays, Canadian (English) – Woman authors*. I. Jansen,
Ann. II. Morningside (Radio program).
PS8309.R34A57 1991   C812/.02208   C91-097175-7
PR9196.7.R34A57 1991

Contents

Introduction, pg vii
White Sand, Judith Thompson, pg 1
Te Pouaka Karaehe: The Glass Box, Renée, pg 29
Venus Sucked In: A Post-feminist Comedy, Anne Chislett, pg 51
Mussomeli–Düsseldorf, Dacia Maraini, pg 79
The Making of Warriors, Sharon Pollock, pg 99
That's Extraordinary!, Diana Raznovich, pg 133

Acknowledgements

My sincere thanks to: Dave Carley, for starting the ball rolling, and for his enthusiastic support in all weathers. The quick-moving Blizzard team. James Roy, for his assistance and patience. Gene Hayden, who was, as always, both encouraging and editorially precise. Deanna Geddo, who translated my interview with Diana Raznovich, and Susana Redondo, for Spanish translation and cheerful help with this and other projects. Margaret Milnes and Suzanne Ellenbogen, for their continued support, editorial and emotional. Sandra Rabinovitch, for introducing me to radio drama, and Bill Lane, for making it possible for me to learn much more. The producers and translators of the six scripts, who took time to talk about their creative choices. And of course, the playwrights, who generously discussed their plays, and made this collection necessary.

Ann Jansen

Introduction

RADIO DRAMA IS AT ONCE an intensely personal and a highly social art. The listener is usually alone with her or his radio, involved in an experience as intimate and direct as the one-to-one relationship between a reader and a novel or a poem on the page. The communication from the writer to the tuned-in ear moves in an almost unwavering line. The producer and composer, actors and musicians, technicians and sound effects people are part of the collective that aims the writer's words through mono or stereo speakers. But the translation of the play from the page to the air is done through very few filters; the words from the playwright's pen move directly toward the hearer. Theatre critic and long-time BBC radio drama producer Martin Esslin wrote of this as the "almost telepathic transference of images from mind to mind." Voices whisper or cajole, shout or sing—intimately, immediately—for you alone.

At the same time, there is an invisible, inaudible crowd tuned in to that transference, an audience of thousands of minds. The experience is individual; it is also shared with a host of others. Most people no longer listen as they once did, groups or families treating the radio as a kind of communicating fire, flickering with stories and sound pictures. Still, those who listen to a radio drama on the CBC—from ocean to ocean, up and down—hear the same monologue or dialogue at the same time. While listeners may not hear their chuckle or gasp of recognition echoed, there are many others out there responding to that present moment on radio. There's no clapping at the play's end, but an entire community has been drawn together for the space of the drama.

Because of Canada's geographical make-up, such a large and varied community could never gather to see live theatre. The scope and size of radio drama audiences, of the Morningside Drama audience in particular, are astonishing when compared to the usual audiences for fiction, on stage or off. Each Morningside Drama is heard by upwards of 750,000 people. Describing the excitement of being able to reach such a large audience, playwright Judith Thompson estimates that the success of her first play *The Crackwalker* has meant a total of perhaps 30,000 viewers in ten years. Just as people tuned in to Morningside sometimes feel like members of a giant book club or an enormous debating society, its radio drama listeners participate in a far-flung dramatic audience.

The six plays in this anthology did a great deal to map out those connections across distances. They were commissioned by Morningside Drama to salute the Second International Women Playwrights Conference, which brought writers from more than thirty countries to Toronto in May 1991. A year prior to the conference, the program's Executive Director, James Roy, and Script Editor, Dave Carley, decided it would be fitting—and exciting—to have a parallel festival of six radio dramas marking this gathering of women playwrights. As well as giving voice to the imaginations of three top Canadian playwrights, the series would give radio listeners a rare chance to hear dramatic stories and styles from three other countries.

Choosing the Canadians was difficult; the Morningside Drama team decided to invite the three women playwrights who had, to that date, won the Governor General's Award for Drama (English language): Anne Chislett, Sharon Pollock and Judith Thompson. Since then, Ann-Marie MacDonald has also received the award for her play, *Goodnight Desdemona (Good Morning Juliet)*. These three women have produced some of the finest dramatic writing in the country. Choosing writers from the whole world was an even greater challenge, limited somewhat by considering playwrights who had previously written for radio, and whose writing was readily available. Finally, three playwrights widely acclaimed in their own countries were selected: Dacia Maraini from Italy; Diana Raznovich, originally from Argentina and now living in Spain; and New Zealander Renée. Translations of the plays by Maraini and Raznovich were commissioned from Canadian playwrights Margaret Hollingsworth and Rosalind Goldsmith.

The playwrights were given a free rein, asked to write on whatever they wished, keeping in mind the common thread of the Women Playwrights Conference. They were also given a half-hour of airtime. Most of Morningside's dramas consist of five episodes of fifteen minutes each; the longer format gave each playwright more time and space. This series was a departure for CBC Radio Drama in other ways. The opportunity to showcase Canadian work alongside that of writers from different countries is infrequent and noteworthy. Occasionally, an English-language production purchased from the BBC or the ABC gives listeners a taste of British or Australian perspectives. But time and budgetary restrictions make it rare for the Radio Drama department to commission original plays from writers outside Canada, especially when translation is in-

Introduction ix

volved. Even theatre-goers have a hard time getting first-hand access to dramatic developments from other countries. Entire worlds of radio drama are unavailable to the most avid listener of plays on the CBC, which is the main producer of the art form in North America.

A commonplace of radio drama is its ability to travel, to leap mountains at a single bound, to move in the blink of an ear between centuries and countries, meadows and mines, the inside of a head and the outside of a universe. Even before getting on air, these plays undertook long journeys. Faxes to Italy, letters to New Zealand, phone calls to Calgary were all part of the process of steering the plays to final drafts that make use of radio's many resources in dramatically different ways. Both serious and comic (although Raznovich asks, "What else exists besides comedy?"), the plays explore diverse climates, both emotional and actual. They employ very different techniques in their "three-dimensional storytelling," as British author Angela Carter terms radio drama. Using radio drama's four elements—speech, silence, sound effects and song/music—the plays move fluidly from present time to flashback, from one character's musings to multi-faceted dialogue, from busy sound collages to silence.

In *White Sand*, Judith Thompson reaches deep into the hearts of her characters. Carl is a skinhead warrior who is willing to fight to keep Canada white, and to organize others for an all-out "war." His girlfriend Kimberly is less sure, but she is pulled into a maelstrom of anger and violence. Velma, a nanny from the West Indies, tries to decipher a portent of disaster as she cares for Eleanor, a spirited child. Thompson has never shied away from intensity; like her other plays, *White Sand* gives no quarter, portraying each character on his or her own terms, extremes which become all too believable. Set in a near-future Toronto, this play is a shocking, but not surprising, depiction of how Canada's simmering racial tensions might erupt. Only months after the play's first airing, race-related riots in Montreal and Halifax showed just how tenuous our kinder, gentler society really is.

The drama opens with two voices intercut in increasingly short bursts: Carl calls for violent action and Velma speaks of her hopes for landed immigrant status and of some unfathomed dread. Less frenetically interspersed scenes follow: Velma in the home of the Dixons and Kimberly in prison years later giving an interview, along with newscasts adding up the body toll. The contrast between the kitchen scenes, with Velma's smooth voice responding to Eleanor's many questions, and the meetings of neo-Nazis held by Carl's hypnotic voice is chilling. Kimberly's descriptions of Carl's tenderness do nothing to dissipate the feeling of dread, the sense of an inexorable movement toward confrontation, toward loss. Toward the play's end, the action intensifies again, numerous short scenes notching the level of tension higher and tighter.

Thompson describes *White Sand* in terms of music and rhythms, and certainly its effectiveness comes in large part from its pacing. The music composed for the production was used to underscore emotionally charged moments, to build towards the final conflagration, but the use of voices is also inherently musical. One of the strongest elements of radio drama is the monologue, that direct, intimate link between a single speaker and a single listener. In this play there are few scenes in dialogue, many involving a solitary voice. Thompson's trademark of monologues that cut to the core is used to great effect in this play, which rests on four strong and very different voices speaking of their fears and hopes.

"I thought somehow I was safe here, that Canada was like the sunny tip of a giant iceberg floatin' in a dark and bleedin' sea, but now it seems, the sea is risin'," says Velma. Kimberly talks of being worn down by the memory of an expression: "*That* is wearin' me down, right? Like the way water does a rock? You ever seen that? Wear it right down to sand, man, right down to white sand." Each character has a distinct voice, instruments played on for the dramatic composition. Yet, the play is much more than a series of monologues, a string of points of view. As producer James Roy puts it, the play's single-voice scenes are so rapidly intercut that the monologues effectively enter into a dialogue with each other. Characters who meet only at the play's end, and then wordlessly, are in communication.

This juxtaposition of scenes, in place of the more usual character interplay, gives *White Sand* much of its dramatic impact. Roy describes the play as extremely dense, a drama that uses radio to its fullest and engages the audience through structure as well as story. "It really got under our skin, the cast, the technical people, because the undercurrent of the play is so grotesque. It creeps up and eats away at you," he says. *White Sand* is anything but comfortable drama. It strips away everything but the essential, moving inexorably to that dreadful moment when the characters collide, when violence screams out and one voice is silenced.

The tone of Renée's *Te Pouaka Karaehe: The Glass Box* is gentle, lyrical. The play depicts a woman caught between two cultures and lifestyles. The main character, a young Maori career woman, is Elizabeth in the city, Irihapeti in Takitimu, her homeland: in one world she is a high-powered civil servant, in the other, she feels an outsider. On returning to Takitimu for the funeral of her grandmother, a great Maori teacher and guide, Elizabeth is torn over how to connect the fragmented pieces of her life. As she tells her sister, her nightmare is about being locked in a glass box, trapped in the maze of the city.

Elizabeth's return is depicted dramatically: her questioning of her heritage comes out through scenes with her family and a friend. Her dilemma is also fleshed out through internal musings and memories. Following in a character's slipstream as she slides between times or silently interjects her feelings into the moment are among the greatest pleasures of radio drama. The listener often has the inside edge. Although Elizabeth is clearly the main player in *Te Pouaka Karaehe*, the play is not restricted to her point of view. In one scene, her sister Wiki's perspective is made clear as she talks to her baby while driving to the airport—of course, the baby gets a few moments of airtime during the journey. And scenes from their past, from memory, are dramatized; Nanny's voice is heard across the years as clearly as the characters speaking in the present. Flashbacks are another satisfying element of radio drama: characters exist the second they speak, and memory becomes real instantaneously.

This play is the first Renée has written with Maori characters in main roles. Of Maori and Scottish ancestry, Renée was brought up in a European tradition and learned about her mother's people late in her life. She says that Elizabeth's dilemma is in some ways the reverse side of her own experience: "too light for some, too dark for others." On her way to the *tangi* or funeral, Elizabeth calls herself a "brown *Pakeha*;" *Pakeha* is the word used by New Zealanders, Maori and white alike, for people of European background. Renée unobtrusively lets an audience far from New Zealand know the Maori terms of reference, as when Nanny's sister speaks: "My sister's spirit is waiting to fly to the place where the waters meet, where our *tupuna* are waiting to gather her in. Oh how will I bear this lonely time until I too am called to be with the old ones! Sit here, Irihapeti, and you too Wiki, here we will wait for her spirit to reach Cape Reinga." Listening to this play on Morningside, thousands of Canadians were introduced to ancient Maori beliefs and to contemporary concerns: the spirits continue to journey to New Zealand's northernmost point even as the survivors struggle to maintain a cultural identity in the anonymous city.

In some ways, this story translates immediately for Canadian listeners, Native or *Pakeha*. Yet, as producer Gregory Sinclair learned, there is a danger in assuming a too-close correspondence between circumstances of First Nations people in the two countries. A Maori lawyer living in Toronto came into the studio to give advice on pronunciations for actors from Australia and Canada; she explained that Maoris are generally much more accepted and successful in New Zealand than Natives are in

Canada. Still, this material success doesn't mitigate the great cultural losses accompanying gains in prestige or power. To underline these cultural differences, Sinclair laced the play with Maori music, both authentic laments and chants, and tunes modernized by synthesizers and computer underscoring. The two styles of music highlight Elizabeth's confusion between two cultures and two worlds: city and country, traditional and modern.

The conflict in Anne Chislett's *Venus Sucked In: A Post-feminist Comedy* is between generations of women in another particular place, a mid-town Toronto apartment. The tone is light and the pacing quick in this comedy about a half-hour in the lives of four female characters: seventeen-year-old Kathy, her mother Liz, her Aunt Bev and her grandmother Betty. The play opens with Kathy rehearsing, out loud, a speech for next day's school. The topic? "Women in the Ninties." Over the course of a Sunday afternoon, her reluctant research includes the inner workings of a dishwasher, the nature of art, Aunt Bev's "perfect" relationship and her own feelings about her parents' break-up. The title comes from one of Liz's paintings, abandoned for the day when Kathy's aunt and grandmother arrive: instead of Venus rising on the half-shell, Liz's version has the love goddess about to be swallowed whole by an oyster.

Venus Sucked In is a classically neat play that observes the unities of time and space, at least on radio's terms. The action takes place in real time, without shifts in tense, and in a realistic space, save for Kathy's speeches. Chislett says she wanted to sidestep radio's famed ease of movement through time and space, to contain the drama in the small space lived by the main character and her mother. "I wanted to do twenty-five minutes with no pyrotechnics, no fancy footwork, just the words," she says. In studio, producer Heather Brown organized the taping, except for Kathy's internals and speeches, in a set-up approximating an apartment, with a few cut corners. The actors moved from space to space as the action shifted, rather than staying with one microphone set-up. Much of the sound was mixed "on the fly," effects achieved as the actors performed. A fridge doubled as dishwasher and the distinct sound of the apartment intercom was created during the performance, not assembled later and laid onto the actors' voices. The result of such "live effects" can be a great match between voices and action; the risk is never being able to adjust the sound once the take is recorded.

Although the script of *Venus Sucked In* reads very much like a stage play, Kathy's speechifying and the fact that the play is presented from the point of view of only one character make it much more subjective than any stage play. In the theatre, viewers can look where they will—they can close their eyes if they like. Radio can direct the listener's attention in a much more focussed way. The story is told entirely from Kathy's perspective; each listener travels *with* Kathy to her new conclusions about the roles of the women in her life. The actor playing Kathy was fitted with a body mike, as well as being recorded with the three other actors on studio mikes. So listeners hear with Kathy's ears, accompany Kathy as she buzzes her grandmother in from downstairs, as she banters with her aunt and baits her mum—as the details of one Sunday afternoon unfold. We eavesdrop with Kathy on the other side of that flimsy apartment door just as we eavesdrop on her speeches.

The production relied on this "realism" and on the balance of four, very different women's voices. Where many radio dramas use music to bridge scenes and provide atmosphere, music was used in *Venus Sucked In* only at the play's beginning and end. Brown describes how refreshing she found this return to some of radio drama's other strengths. Many radio dramas are very technically created, fully exploiting the medium's ability to go anywhere and do anything through sound. "It's good to remember that radio drama is really about language and words and thoughts," says Brown.

Like Chislett's play, *Mussomeli–Düsseldorf* takes place in real time and uses few fancy radio flourishes. The forward momentum in Dacia Maraini's play comes partly from the train journey being taken by its two main characters. An Italian mother and daughter are travelling from their home farm in Sicily to the German city. Although her husband has been working in Düsseldorf for many years, while living with another woman and their children, the mother has remained faithful—but her daughter sets out to change that. The third character, a ticket collector, enters their train compartment and the drama, interrupting the women as they play at cards and disagree about life and love. The play contains only these three characters: a rural woman who holds to the old ways, a seventeen-year-old who challenges her mother's every belief and a man willing to go along for the ride.

"You only get one husband—one husband and one soul," says the mother early in the game. Why remain faithful to a husband rarely seen, the daughter argues, trying to shock her mother with her own liberal ideas on marriage and abortion. "Mamma, sometimes you sound like you came out of the ark," she says, and when the mother sidesteps this, saying "Oh come on, play, throw out that seven of clubs you're holding—," she responds with, "How did you know I have the seven?" "Oh," says her mother, "we have good memories in the ark." The sexual skirmish that begins with the arrival of the ticket collector at first seems to provide a bridge between the two women, but it is merely fodder for the continuing contest between old and young, faithful and rebellious.

There are no scene shifts; only the entry of the ticket collector breaks into the ebb and flow of the mother-and-daughter talk, which goes beyond card moves to a generational clash at times fervent, at times running in a well-worn track. The movement of the train, the sense of a journey travelled uncountable times along an unchanging route, underlines the repetitive nature of their disagreement. The train pauses and continues; its rhythms an aural backdrop for the talk within the compartment. The train becomes a kind of fourth character, its momentum interacting with the push and pull of two conflicting viewpoints.

The central circumstance of this play, migrant husbands working in far-off cities and countries, has been an important reality in Italy. Men leave Sicilian farms for a wage elsewhere, wives turn into grass widows and their daughters dream of city ways. Maraini describes the themes of her play as immigration and the conflict between two cultures and generations: the traditional, regional culture of the mother and the emancipated, modern culture of the daughter. The older holds to the advice of the Madonna, to the constancy of the moon; the younger is eager for change and a different kind of motion. As their journey continues Maraini refuses to weight the argument on one side or the other, or to reach any one conclusion. The playwright's sympathy for both characters is apparent; their debate is nuanced and many-tiered, their feeling for each other the real drive behind continuing the conversation, the card game, the journey.

The translator and producer of this drama had to find a way to interpret a play that in Italian is somewhat mannered, with characters who are sometimes lively and engaged, but also has a stylized, almost abstract quality. "There's a slightly formal, slightly ironic underpinning to what she writes," said Margaret Hollingsworth. "She's writing lushly, romantically, using stereotypes that aren't really stereotypes. Nothing is ever quite as it seems—that's very Italian." In translating the drama, Hollingsworth had difficulty finding Canadian colloquialisms to equal the sometimes very earthy Italian, specifically Sicilian, phrases. One of the cultural referents, the card game, simply resisted translation. Producer Kathleen Flaherty, who learned how to play *scopa* before directing the drama, describes its playing style as very boisterous and excitable; she can think of no equivalent for the game's strategies in Canadian cardplaying. The impossibility of translating this central metaphor points up the general challenge of performing and producing a play across cultures.

In *The Making of Warriors*, Sharon Pollock deals with two centuries of assaults on women and asks her audience for a direct response. Interweaving events from two lives, this complex drama draws parallels between the conditions that have oppressed or endangered women across two centuries. It also questions how history is recreated, taking on the issue of how to tell stories of losses and gains from any one perspective. At first glance, the two stories are far removed from each other. Sarah Moore Grimke was an American who died in 1873, at the age of 81, after a lifetime of fighting for women's rights; she is now virtually forgotten. Anna Mae Pictou Aquash was a Micmac and a Native rights activist murdered in 1976, under circumstances that have yet to be satisfactorily explained. Although the dates and circumstances of these two women differ greatly, the causes and consequences of their oppression are frighteningly similar. While researching the two women's lives, Pollock discovered that much of the language used to justify women's limited roles in the nineteenth century echoes the phrasing of current discussions about self-government and aboriginal rights.

Pollock made strikingly different choices when she set about presenting the two lives. She uses a traditional dramatic style for the earlier story, a combination of storytelling and fact-finding for the second. Both stories involve narration; *The Making of Warriors* is a good example of how writers use narration in radio drama to draw an audience in or to hold it at a remove. Between dramatizations of scenes from different periods in Sarah Moore Grimke's life one of the three unnamed women narrators, Woman Three, recites details of her story. Anna Mae Pictou Aquash never enters the drama as speaker. Instead, her life and her death are described by two women who directly address the listener. She is realized in the drama only through the words of others, who try to make sure her story is heard.

In her youth in Charleston, South Carolina, Sarah Moore Grimke defied the law by teaching slaves to read; in her old age, she strove to get across the message of suffrage. Born into an upper-class, slave-owning family, she drew the comparison between being a woman and being a slave: "I comprehend what bein' a slave means! It means no education so a person can't defend herself, or earn a livin' or maintain an independent income, it means not controllin' the basic decisions a your life, and no legal recourse to right wrongs or injustices, that's what it means!" From her public speaking, through her mid-life silencing, to her return to activism, Sarah's history is presented dramatically; we hear the people and understand the events contributing to the shape of her life.

We learn the "facts" of Anna Mae Pictou Aquash's life by different means. Woman One, who describes herself as a middle-class white woman, talks about driving through the Pine Ridge Reserve in South Dakota on February 24th, 1976. Her tone is confiding, personal. As the drama circles back again and again to her small part of the story, a disturbing picture of what she saw on the highway emerges. Woman Two's brisk, reportorial voice outlines recorded events; she builds a case for the official intimidation and state-sanctioned killing of this woman and others involved with the American Indian Movement in the 1970s. Together the two voices establish, through a balance of subjective and objective descriptions, the details of a brutally shortened life.

The three narrative voices act as a chorus linking the stories of the two activists. The play begins with all three speaking together; an overlapping repetition of the words "the making of warriors" is followed by three separate descriptions of the drama to come as "an exploration of, a story about, a personal reminiscence." In the final moments of the play, the three women provide a summation. They also issue a direct challenge: Remember, as we have been remembering, and act. Pollock's political will is as evident as her sophisticated use of dramaturgy in this play.

The Making of Warriors moves surely between the confined circumstances of Sarah Moore Grimke and the descriptions of Anna Mae Pictou Aquash's committed and curtailed life. The cool tones of a harpsichord counterpoint Sarah's efforts within a restricted environment; Native drumming and chanting underlie the increasingly urgent recall of the onlookers of Anna Mae's life. Though most of the voices in the play are women's, they are clearly differentiated. As described by producer James Roy, Woman One is warm, down-to-earth; Woman Two, determined, even driven; and Woman Three, classy, genteel, in keeping with the time of her story. The mixture of narrative voices and dramatic scenes was specifically designed for the Morningside context: Pollock consciously chose to emphasize elements that show up on any given day on the program, single-voice storytelling, current affairs techniques and dramatization.

Through writing *The Making of Warriors* in this way, Pollock poses a number of difficult questions about writing dramas based on historical abuses of power. How does a writer remind people of injustice, work to right wrongs, tell a story? Particularly when the story is complicated, highly charged and draws on different cultures. One of Pollock's concerns was that Anna Mae Pictou Aquash's history is so powerful, her death so horrific, that any dramatization might diminish it. And while she wanted to tell both stories, Pollock says she only felt comfortable dramatizing the one closer to her own experience, though further removed in time. Introducing three women to tell three different stories was a way of making her perspective clear. Pollock identifies herself with the fifty-four-year-old white woman who catches only a glimpse of what happened to the murdered Native woman.

Pollock's concern about telling tales from other cultures is shared by many in the Canadian literary world and further afield. This debate is particularly pointed for playwrights, whose work can rarely rest on one point of view. However, Pollock's fear of misappropriating the story of another results in one of the play's two central figures never getting a chance to speak. One might argue that this is appropriate, that Anna Mae Pictou Aquash was also silenced by agents of the dominant white culture. Pollock is clear about her intentions, about her "point of entry" in *The Making of Warriors*. Both the dramatization and the documentation lead to greater knowledge of these two women, both have an emotional as well as factual impact. The two lives and deaths are connected by the play as exploration, story and personal reminiscence.

In *That's Extraordinary!*, Diana Raznovich tackles media exploitation in an over-the-top social satire. Her parody of a radio show unmasks the follies of mass addiction to sensational, voyeuristic programming, doing so with great humour and panache. A radio show called "That's Extraordinary!" hypes its latest media coup, an on-site suicide, recorded as it happens. Alicia has decided to kill herself on a mountaintop, not realizing that her final moments are the day's fodder for an intrusive program where the intimacies of life—and now death—are exposed on candid microphones. The play opens with Alicia expressing her final sentiments in a storm, a tender scene abruptly ended by an obnoxiously upbeat radio theme, and by an unctuous host trumpeting the new, live (for now) special: "Suicide on a Hilltop."

Alicia doesn't suspect the program's appropriation, even when a reporter pops up and solicits her last words with his own sob story. Meanwhile, the MC is busy manipulating his audience. He milks every moment, cajoling or bullying his listeners into staying tuned, turning up the suspense with cliff-hanging questions. He also peddles fabricated insights into Alicia's past. At one point he says to Gaspar, the on-the-scene reporter: "We have heard directly her conversations with the wind, the poppies, the sun and God, and I must say it has been stupendous to follow her final emotions at such close range. But our curiosity has no end. Tell us—what does she look like?"

The action is set in radio land rather than any particular country, although the play's exuberant and flamboyant writing and pacing clearly owe something to the writer's knowledge of the media mores of two different countries, Spain and Argentina. The language reaches flowery heights and the action grows more and more extravagant; the production correspondingly played the overblown scenario as larger-than-life and at an almost dizzying pace. Comic timing between the actors playing Gaspar and Alicia was crucial. An unusual casting requirement was that the actor playing Alicia be able to whistle, although the bird- songs could be done on a synthesizer. The soundscape of the hillside, where birds and breezes conspire to alter Alicia's mood, contrasts with the foreground attack of the radio show.

This is certainly brash radio, with no subtle fades between scenes, no tasteful restraint. The MC's purple prose is more than matched by the program's melodramatic sound and music cues. As producer Kathleen Flaherty puts it, she and the technicians put in every "piece of bad radio," every sound cliché they could find: plates drop, doors slam and the wind moans and howls at a high emotional volume. When the MC drops his voice to talk of Alicia's broken heart, a satisfyingly loud crash accompanies his pop psychology. The show's shifts between syrup and suspense are underscored by triumphant marches and romantic melodies, with few holds barred. In keeping with the commentator's use of sports terminology, much of the music was chosen from sports themes, driving and aggressive pieces that push listeners along to the finish line. There the final face-off between Alicia and Gaspar takes a turn even the MC can't smother in flowery phrases.

Collisions between cultures—between generations of women, between women and men, between the powerful and the powerless—are central to these six plays. This theme underlines the importance of the cultural collusion involved in getting them produced and heard across Canada. Serious and irreverent, angry or ironic, these plays present fresh and challenging perspectives on women, on men and on their worlds in transition. They provide an opportunity to hear from six remarkable women dramatists, in a time when women playwrights are still underrepresented on stages around the world. Most exciting, the plays present wonderful casts of female characters. In each drama, women characters are central; in most, there are more female characters than male. This shouldn't be cause for applause, but it is while many cultural offerings continue to present some unknown planet where only twenty percent of the population is female. Here women take first crack at the microphone.

Radio drama is all about voices; these six plays provide an earful of women's voices.

This series provided a rare chance to have radio dramas travel such distances, cover so much ground. This collection is an equally rare opportunity to reflect on the plays' journeys. Radio drama is a notoriously evanescent art: as Canadian playwright George Ryga wrote, "By its very nature, radio is a moment of life instantly committed to memory." Few radio plays are published; fewer are released on cassette. While the stage play varies from production to production and instant to instant, the radio play, though fixed in amber, usually disappears, except in the mind of the hearer, once the program is signed off. While a record of the finished work does exist on tape, contractual arrangements and funding aimed primarily at production mean the CBC rarely markets even its finest radio dramas on cassettes. The keenest listener usually gets only two chances at hearing any drama on the air. If you miss the minimal promotion or aren't tied to a radio at the time of broadcasting, both airings can pass by unheard. It's hard to recommend radio plays to friends when they're over.

And even harder if they're never aired in the first place. Radio drama in Canada is facing ever leaner days. As time slots for drama are whittled away, there is less space to develop writers, to create entire worlds on tape—voice by voice, sound by sound, layer by layer—to produce plays that take time and risks. As these six plays do. And now they have another chance for an audience, a chance to take each of you to far reaches and places as near as your own heart.

Ann Jansen
September 1991

White Sand

by Judith Thompson

2 Airborne: Radio Plays by Women

JUDITH THOMPSON enters familiar terrain in *White Sand*, while mapping out a new configuration of land-mines. In this drama, a skinhead warrior and his girlfriend enter into a horrible trajectory with a peaceful woman from the West Indies. As in her previous plays, life for Thompson's characters is fraught with peril: evil casts a blight on the landscape, and light's dark twin has almost unbearable powers. Thompson's interest in the powers of evil shapes the play, as does her belief that something in the human spirit strives to withstand these forces. Though the conflict is monumental, it's also an everyday event that takes place under the most banal circumstances.

"There's this gentle lady, Velma, struggling in her way and here's this enormous ego, Carl, struggling in his way," Thompson says of two of the play's characters. "They collide, like a comet and a planet. There's a terrible inevitability about the collision. You know, you can be getting on your coat and meanwhile, these skinheads are preparing for something terrible and you don't know, and you have a hot dog and then suddenly you're dead. And that's what interests me. Who might enter your life or mine, tonight, today, tomorrow?

"I guess it's my belief that there's this huge ocean of evil in everybody, that if you open the door it's just waiting. There's no evil in a one-year-old, I know that. It starts at three. That's when they can hurt somebody; they can wall off and separate themselves from what they're doing. I wish it wasn't there, I hope that it's not there, but I do have this horrible feeling, this fear that it is there for everybody."

Thompson drew on many sources in constructing this collision. When she talks about the play, images from films on My Lai tumble out alongside details from newspaper reports of violence closer to home. Documentaries on Stalin, Hitler and Mao made Thompson ponder the power of oratory, "the hypnotic power of the word, which is very appropriate for radio." Considering someone like Hitler, who was initially dismissed by German intellectuals as a fool, Thompson thought about how impossible it is to isolate the elements of such hypnotic power: "It's like a beautiful face that's really quite ugly—you can't separate any of the features. With all the flaws, it is only what it is when they're put together. It's chemistry, and of course force of conviction."

Thompson began to think of Canada and of gangs of skinheads who hang out in a park near her Toronto home. She describes Carl, the gang leader in *White Sand*, as someone who picks up phrases on the news, tidbits that make him sound clever, and also has an instinct for what incites people. "No matter how left-wing you are, it really does bother you if you've been trying to get a job for so many years and somebody walks into the country and takes it," says Thompson. Although Carl starts off as a "goof," someone who can be brushed off, he begins to prey on fears and issues that everybody might agree with a little—and then explodes them.

Thompson describes Carl's girlfriend, who might just as easily have been Velma's friend, as someone who is simply taking care of her needs. "I wanted to explore all that, how Kimberly could have knowledge, have sympathy, and yet do what she has to do," says Thompson. "She's been taught that being in love with a man is the be-all and the end-all, and so she obsesses. I guess it must be the survival instinct, that's why it's so strong and overcomes so many convictions. I would say that love-obsession wins much more than convictions or ideas do."

Carl's genius lies in his ability to make the world come alive for people around him, to cut through the dead layers with which people protect themselves as a means of survival. Carl lives on the edge and feels more, and he is able to translate his rage to others around him. "Rage is something we all have. It's not evil or good, it's just there, a huge power," says Thompson. "I don't know what it is, I just like to explore it. Rage is the power in everybody. If you can find someone's rage, you can find their power."

The gentler side of the drama comes from the characters of Velma and Eleanor. Velma is based loosely on the West Indian woman who helps care for Thompson's three children, and on her experience of trying to become a Canadian citizen. Thompson describes Velma as a woman at peace with herself, despite being troubled by her children living in another country. Although Velma feels her brother was exploited by his "flat mate," she isn't consciously homophobic says Thompson. "Music is what gives Velma comfort and how she gives the little girl, Eleanor, comfort," says Thompson. "Music is like the light, it's like the angel, it's the good. It's God, I guess, coming through."

Any hope in the play comes from this connection between Velma and the child. "The little girl seems to me to be something of a hero," says Thompson. "There's a possibility for heroism later in life for her." But the force of violence that grows through the drama makes the light seem tenuous, very threatened. Neither her religion nor her music protect Velma. "That's what's horrifying, she's not protected by her song. It's all so random," says Thompson. "The sad and negative thing is that I did leave Kimberly hard at the end. She'll go back to Carl. And he's going to do it again. He's coming back."

The play's structure is very concentrated, built on rhythms Thompson describes in terms of music, with an intense crescendo as the play concludes. "Near the end, it was as much the form as the content that moved me, in a sort of visceral, physical way," says Thompson about listening to the play on radio. The four voices touch different chords in the listener: "Velma has to be like velvet, musical and calm. Eleanor has to be this bright sound, like a robin in the spring. Kimberly has to be a mixture of a healthy young girl and someone aged. Even when she's young there has to be just a stain of the hardness, the deadness she had to have to do what she did. And the stain just got bigger and bigger and bigger.

"Carl's voice has to be somehow hypnotic. It has to envelop. You know how you want some people to keep on talking because you just love to be enveloped in their voice. He's saying things that make people feel something. A lot of people are used to going from breakfast and lunch to dinner without feeling anything, and people who make them feel are very exciting. They'll follow them to the ends of the earth."

Except for one scene between Carl and Kimberly, the only real dialogue is between Velma and the child. The rest of the writing consists of heart-stopping monologues. Thompson is frank about her love of the monologue form and her corresponding love of writing for radio. "In monologues, it all comes gushing out, like a geyser," she says. "On radio, plays with too much subtext can get boring because you can't see the actors' faces. Radio is a place where people say what they mean. That's what I like about radio—I'm not into subtlety.

"I like this idea of voices in the dark, whispering; schizophrenics hear voices in the dark, it affects them deeply. The voice and you—I just love that, no distractions. It's a pure experience. I don't like dialogue on radio much. I get bored at the sound of the doorbell and 'How was your day?' ... 'Oh, not too bad' ... I just get distracted, but not when there's one voice. There's dialogue in *White Sand*, but they're not really talking to each other.

"I think radio is about poetry, because poetry is about rhythm, word choice. It's something that actually *carves* into you, the poetry and the word choice. That's what radio should do, carve into you, make those big holes like in the wheat, the circles. That's what it should do, and mostly it doesn't, but sometimes it does. I was pleased with *White Sand*—I felt it cut a swath."

JUDITH THOMPSON was born in Montreal in 1954 and grew up in Connecticut and Ontario. She received her BA from Queen's University in Kingston, Ont. and graduated from the acting program of the National Theatre School. *The Crackwalker*, her first play, premièred at Toronto's Theatre Passe Muraille in 1980, and was a finalist in both the Clifford E. Lee playwrighting competition and the National Repertory Theatre Play Awards. It has since been produced across Canada and in the United States, Israel and Australia. She has twice won the Governor General's Award for Drama: in 1984 for *White Biting Dog*, and in 1989 for a collection of plays titled *The Other Side of the Dark*, which includes *I Am Yours*, winner of the Chalmers Canadian Play Award. She is a long-time playwright-in-residence at Tarragon Theatre in Toronto, which premièred her plays *White Biting Dog* and *I Am Yours*. In 1990, she directed the première of her play *Lion in the Streets* at Tarragon Theatre and the duMaurier Festival in Toronto. She directed her adaptation of *Hedda Gabler* at the Shaw Festival in 1991. Resident in Toronto, she also writes for radio, television and film. Her radio dramas include *A Big White Light, Quickening, A Kissing Way* and *Tornado*, which received a Nellie for Best Radio Drama in 1988.

Characters

CARL   skinhead warrior, thirty
VELMA   Caribbean nanny, regal, but uneducated, middle-aged
KIMBERLY   Carl's girlfriend, at ages eighteen and thirty-one
ELEANOR   a bright child
NEWSCASTER, CROWD

Production Credits

White Sand was commissioned by the Canadian Broadcasting Corporation for Morningside Drama and first broadcast on the CBC Radio network on May 24, 1991.

CARL   Stephen Ouimette
VELMA   Denise Jones
KIMBERLY   Jane Spidell
ELEANOR   Lisa Boynton
NEWSCASTER   David Huband

Produced and directed in Toronto by James Roy, Executive Producer of Morningside Drama. Orginal music by Bill Thompson. Casting Consultant: Linda Grearson. Recording Engineer: Glen McLaughlin. Sound effects by Matt Willcott. Production Assistant: Nina Callaghan. Script Editor: Dave Carley.

White Sand

Scene One

(MUSIC: Theme; fades underneath.)

(SOUND: Bar. Background voices in bar. CARL, a neo-Nazi, has an extremely rich and resonant voice. Occasional sound of small, rapt audience.)

CARL: My name ... is Carl ... I *am* Canadian ... and I *want* my country ... back. Do you? Do *you*? Do *you*? Do *you* want *your* country? Or are ya happy to watch them ... suck it away. The "wretched," the "starving," the so-called refugees, the immi-*grunts* who would cut your throat soon as look at you, they hate you, man.

Scene Two

(Kitchen.)

(SOUND: Washing dishes. Baby gurgling in background. Birds outside window.)

VELMA: *(Sings.)* Mango mango mango vey, mango teen, mango do do's, soo-tey ma-tan; tey tey bo ... all for me ... mango mango ... mango vey mango teen ... *(Fades underneath.)*

Scene One (continued)

(Bar.)

(SOUND: As before.)

CARL: *(Continues after one line of song.)* They ... hate ... you with all their guts, man, they call our women "sluts," they-come-here-with-a-plan, you seen 'em, wide-eyed and covered in phony scars they done themselves, saying they're, like, running away from Communists; and in case you didn't know it, the ones that run Immigration in this country are Communists, a bunch of Communistic faggots. Yes sir, Stalin, it's vicious red queers hold the keys to our country, a legacy of the biggest red queer of all, Mr. Fuddle Duddle, but they do, oh yeah, yes they are ushering in our enemies, termites, like themselves, who will chew and chew away the fabric of our dear country. I have asked you here tonight, to put a stop to this.

Scene Two (continued)

(Kitchen.)

(SOUND: As before.)

VELMA: *(Internal.)* My eye beatin' today, from early mornin', I well wonderin' what that mean. I call Cecile in Brooklyn and she say everything fine; her husband still have the lung cancer but he don't know he have it so his spirits is not bad, then after I calls Trinidad and Nicole say, "No, everything fine, Mummy, why do you worry so much?" and then, I lookin' at the picture of Michael on my bureau, and it seem he speakin' to me from the dead.

Scene One (continued)

(Bar.)

(SOUND: As before. Big laugh from CARL's audience and some twitters.)

CARL: No, tell me about it, Derek, you seen Chinatown Friday? One minute they're sittin' in there eatin' chicken-fried rice and then next they're starin' at a plate of Vietnam brains. Hey you, Laurie, bring me another round of Canadians and put it on my tab. Man, the gook who did the shootin'? He was behind bars in Hong Kong for multiple murders, right? And our faggot friends with the keys thought it'd be a really good idea if he came and lived here for a while! Ya gotta hand it to 'em man—

Scene Two (continued)

(Kitchen.)

(SOUND: As before.)

VELMA: *(Internal.)* The last time my eye beatin' on the bus to Immigration. It didn't make any sense that day either, because I felt so well, I knew I looked very nice, wearin' my long yellow dress with my daffodil yellow head scarf, I knew I made a definite impression, and yellow always good for business affairs, this always true, and yet, my eye beatin'. My left eye, same as today.

Scene One (continued)

(Bar.)

(SOUND: As before.)

CARL: Take a walk through the socialist nightmare, Metro Subsidized Housing, where Toronto's diarrhea likes to meet, *see who is sucking the tit of our country, sucking it ... cracked* and *dry*, listen, listen to me, I walked through Regent's Park with my buddies the other night—call it reconnaissance—and we did not see a white face. Not one white face—just cockroaches doing drug deals—*these scum do not pay a cent for their homes,* their housing is free! *Free!* and who do ya think *pays* for their housing? *Me! You! Us dumb white Canadians* who are stupid enough to work for a living, they're laughing up their noses at us my friends, we *break our backs* every day from dawn to dark so that black and brown *scum* can sit on their *butts* in donut shops waitin' on their pusher so they can spend the bucks they save on rent *on crack*. They got their women whorin' on the street, some of our women too, I don't mind telling you, but we'll get to that later, they let their children run wild, they *sucker* the state and then spend their life stoned. *You* work on the highways, the building sites, in the dark factories, and the abattoirs to keep these ... "people" stoned?

Scene Two (continued)

(Kitchen.)

(SOUND: As before.)

VELMA: *(Internal.)* Well, I had bad news that day man, and the whole month follow like that.

(SOUND: No ambient sound in the following scenes. Near the end more overlap between the speakers is possible.)

Scene One (continued)

(Bar.)

CARL: Something is wrong with this picture.

Scene Two (continued)

(Kitchen.)

(SOUND: Baby crying, then being calmed down by a bottle, but it is all very distant.)

VELMA: *(Internal, preoccupied.)* The whole month follow like that, with the worst news of my life, it come at the end.

Scene One (continued)

(Bar.)

(MUSIC: Begins and continues underneath.)

CARL: Let us send them a missile; a message of force.

Scene Two (continued)

(Kitchen.)

VELMA: *(Internal.)* I hear that now one ham cost more than one hundred dollars in Trinidad.

Scene One (continued)

(Bar.)

CARL: *You are not wanted here!*

Scene Two (continued)

(Kitchen.)

VELMA: *(Internal.)* I will be very disappointed if they don't let me stay. I want to bring my three daughters here, and live a nice, quiet life.

Scene One (continued)

(Bar.)

CARL: *(Near tears.)* We do not want you hanging on the nipple of our great country, clawing her lovely face, and and ...

Scene Two (continued)

(Kitchen.)

VELMA: *(Internal.)* I wonder if this is what it means. I will be very disappointed if I am deported at the end of this month.

Scene One (continued)

(Bar.)

CARL: ... making her tired, man. My mother died of cancer when I was twelve, up till then I was, you know, little bow tie, top marks in the class, teacher's pet, up on Mummy's knee—then I saw this great lady tired, sucked dry by by ... serving hamburgers every day to them, gettin' no tips from *them*, having her ass pinched by *them*, I seen her throw up green, and ...

Scene Two (continued)

(Kitchen.)

VELMA: *(Internal.)* I do everything right for them, I live in with the Dixons, though it give me no privacy whatsoever, I takin' the health care aide course all Saturday every Saturday, I even doin' the volunteer work at the home for the aged, what more can they want from me?

Scene One (continued)

(Bar.)

CARL: That night I punched three holes in the drywall with my head. Ask my brothers.

Scene Two (continued)

(Kitchen.)

VELMA: *(Internal.)* My children have very little chances there, for ... upgrading.

Scene One (continued)

(Bar.)

CARL: Our great, stooping country is swaying! Swaying in this savage wind, weakened, by parasites—

Scene Two (continued)

(Kitchen.)

VELMA: If the first time my eye beatin' it a forecastin'—of my own brother's death—

Scene One (continued)

(Bar.)

CARL: Sickened by their greed, their carnivorous need, we must save our mother!

Scene Two (continued)

(Kitchen.)

VELMA: If I am deported, I will never be the same.

Scene One (continued)

(Bar.)

CARL: *(Whisper.)* We must save our mother.

(MUSIC: Ends.)

Scene Two (continued)

(Kitchen.)

VELMA: *(Sings.)* Mango mango mango vey, mango teen, mango do do's, soo-tey ma-tan; tey tey bo ... all for me ... mango mango ... mango vey mango teen ...

Scene Three

(Bathroom.)

(SOUND: Water splashing in bath.)

KIMBERLY: *(At age 18. In the bath.)* Yesterday he come down I'm sittin' in the kitchen with Dawn, eh, playin' cards?

(MUSIC: Creeps in underneath.)

And he goes, "Let me see your hands"—haven't seen him for two weeks 'cause a his campaign thing and that's the first thing he says to me—so I show him my hands and he goes down on his knees and he starts to cry. That's the kind of guy he is. See, I admit it, I do bite my nails, on account of my nerves: my Mum bites hers too; with my sister, Charlene, it's so bad some days she can't pick nothin' up—it's a family trait, we got bad nerves—least I don't smoke, or eat like some pig, I just—chew my nails—well, now the tips of my fingers 'cause I don't got no nails left to chew—and I guess they are kinda bleedin' right now a bit—I never seen a guy cry before—but Carl, I'm tellin' ya, Carl isn't like no other guy I ever went out with. Not only does he cry—and he cries, man, not just at my nails but at like a beautiful tree, or something sad in the paper, like about a kid, big tears make his face all wet—what was I sayin'? Oh yeah, see Carl is on this earth for a reason. And ... what was it he said? Oh yeah, um ... everyone shall know his name. See, what he says is he's givin' his life to uh ... public service—and ... it's his ... destiny.

(MUSIC: Ends.)

Scene Four

(Kitchen.)

(SOUND: VELMA is cleaning up and making dessert.)

ELEANOR: *(Sings.)* Daisy, Daisy give me your answer true, I'm half crazy, all for the loooove—

VELMA: *(Off.)* Eleanor, no singin' at the table, you heard your Mummy tell you that!

ELEANOR: I can if I want.

VELMA: *(Off.)* Eleanor Dixon, I don't like backtalk.

ELEANOR: *Velma!*

VELMA: *(Moving on.)* Yes, I'm right here, you don't have to yell!

ELEANOR: What's wrong with your eye?

VELMA: You eat your dinner, child.

ELEANOR: Not until you tell me what's wrong with your eye.

VELMA: Eleanor, if you keep talkin' to me like that I will have to tell your Mummy.

ELEANOR: Yesterday morning? When you weren't here? I said I hated my Harvest Crunch so Mummy threw the whole bowl in the garbage.

VELMA: Don't go tellin' tales.

ELEANOR: It's true. Then she started to cry and said that nobody liked anything about her. Especially Daddy.

VELMA: *(Moving off.)* I don't want to hear things like that, child. Eat your dinner.

ELEANOR: If they got divorced, I'd go with Mummy half the time and Daddy the other half. 'Cause there's good things about both of them.

VELMA: *(Moving on.)* You don't have to worry, Elly, your parents will not get divorced. I know that.

ELEANOR: How? How do you know?

VELMA: Some things I know.

ELEANOR: Mummy says you're super ... super ... sss ... super something.

VELMA: Superstitious. You can tell your Mummy that I have never seen a thirteenth floor in any buildin' in this country. This ... advanced ... and sophisticated country. *All* people is superstitious. And *all* superstitions is right.

ELEANOR: I have one, I think, only one *real* supersession and that is ... that I don't want to get *any* older than I am *this* second. And if I close my eyes *really really* hard, so hard that it hurts, I can stay exactly the same.

VELMA: *(Internal.)* Superstitious. Man, she is really somethin', to tell a child a thing like that. What about her? With four boxes of make-up and it still don't make her face bright. Lord give me mercy it feel like a green frog try to jump out of my eyelid. What will happen now?

Scene Three (continued)

(Bathroom.)

(SOUND: As before.)

KIMBERLY: *(At age 18. In the bath.)* It's hard on him, you know, like he never sleeps, he has to go out just about every night to meetings and rallies, the cops are always after him—sometimes he don't even want sex. He never let me come to one of his speeches yet, he says it's too much politic stuff, and I hate politics, man, he *knows* I do. When he turns on the news? I get into the bath or call up Charlene. I'm not sittin' there watchin' him yell at the TV ... no way Charlie Chan. I'll tell ya the truth, there's only one thing that's been buggin' me—and that is that yesterday? After he was crying and carryin' on about my nails? He tells me to get ready for war. He tells me think of someone tying up and beatin' on my poor old mother; he told me think on that every second of every day, and prepare. Why did he say that? What's this all got to do with my Mum? And how does he know that my Dad takes the hand to her? I never told him. Sometimes I think he's a spook. And what the hell's he talkin' about a war? There hasn't been a war here since 1812!

Scene Five

(Outdoors.)

(SOUND: A milling, excited crowd of about a hundred. The sound dies down quickly when CARL begins to speak.)

CARL: My friends, my comrades, tonight. Tonight let the war begin. Your theatre? Our city. Your mission? In-secticide. *(Laughs.)* I love you, my comrades, my meteors, sacred, avenging rocks, our people are depending upon you, their soldiers to defend their fair city, so *rain! Shoot* out of the dark space to which you have been exiled, and into the light!

(MUSIC: Begins, continues underneath.)

Enter the subways, the buses, the shopping malls, churches, and shatter the enemy now. Those who would bring Canada to her knees, blindfolded and gagged and degrade her. Those who would drown your white children at birth. Those who refuse to speak English, who spit on our mother-tongue even inside her body. Those who spit on our mother-tongue. I exhort you: strike big, so the paper, the television and the radio can shout to the world that the war has begun. So the throngs and throngs of our spiritual allies the silent Canadians will be emboldened, en-couraged! To join us, and win! Do you hear me?

CROWD: *Yes!*

CARL: Do you hear me!

CROWD: *Yes!*

CARL: The time has come! Now!

CROWD: *Now!*

CARL: *Now!*
CROWD: *Now! Now! Nowww!*
(MUSIC: Ends.)

Scene Six

(Bedroom.)
(SOUND: Clatter of large picture falling down.)
VELMA: *(Internal. Gasps.)* Michael's picture fall! He now try to tell me something sure! Michael! Michael, what are you saying, where should I watch?

Scene Seven

(Broadcast.)
NEWSCASTER: *(On radio.)* Last night in Metro, gangs of skinheads went on a rampage that left seven dead and thirty-nine injured. The police believe the incident was racially motivated.... *(Fades into:)*
(SOUND: White noise, becomes loud.)

Scene Eight

(Prison interview room.)
(SOUND: White noise fades underneath and becomes murmur of several background conversations. Occasional clang of steel doors.)
KIMBERLY: *(At age 31.)* I'll tell ya one thing you can write in your article and that is that it was like a roller coaster. Oh yes. I will not deny to your face that it was some fun. I mean ... some ... rush, right? Like, well think of it, right, it's thirteen years ago. I was seventeen, we're gettin' on the Doc Martens and the camouflage pants, we're drunk out of our minds on tequila—Carl's favourite drink so we all drank it, right?—and we're running down Parliament Street like a pack of wild dogs. I never felt so free in my life. That's it. I never felt so free in my life. But then, and you can write this part down right now, do, come on, I don't like just the tape, write it down, I want it down. At first ... when it came to actually doin' ... what Carl was tellin' us to *do*—well, put it this way, do you think you could slaughter your own meat? Like, cut the throat of a cow with big brown eyes? No way, even though it *is* an animal, give me peanut butter on toast for the rest of my life, right? You know what I'm sayin'? So when we got

onto the bus and Derek starts in on this one ... *(Holding back tears.)* old ... gentleman, Chinese I think he was ... and Gavin and Mike and Huntley and everybody ... kicking and ... with the ... baseball bats, and ... well a baseball bat may not do much damage to a ball, but you ever seen ...? Well, anyways, and ... there was like lots of big strong lookin' guys on that bus, even Chinese ones, but do you think anybody came to that old man's help? I'll tell ya the truth, I was actually thinkin' where's them Chinese gangs now, when this old guy needs 'em? I was actually *hopin'*—

(MUSIC: Begins, continues underneath.)

So Darlene starts screamin' at me that I'm a coward and a traitor and she's telling Carl so I go up and slapped the guy's face and then I turned around and went off the bus. And then I sat in a donut shop all night drinkin' coffee 'cause I was too afraid to go home to Carl. Even though I did have the excuse of bein' four months pregnant with his baby, I was too scared to tell Carl. But you know what? He came and got me, I guess one of his spies told him where I was, eh, he came and got me and scooped me up in his arms, and took me home and made the most beautifullest love to me he's ever made. The only thing was, his hands were shakin' the whole time we're doin' it. And every time I seen them, they looked just like the Chinaman's ...

(SOUND: Buzzer.)

I have to go. Now we get to go sit in our cells and think about our sins, right? *Okay okay* I'm comin'! Ya dumb dyke.... They're all dykes you know.

(MUSIC: Ends.)

Scene Nine

(Bedroom.)

VELMA: *(On the phone.)* I know I should go to that meetin', Annette, stop tellin' me that ... I told you I am not the politic type of person! No! No! I tell you I don't like big crowds, it make me dizzy. Yes, always, it always too hot and too crowded I can do nothin' for nobody there. Here in my home, I pray, and I write down my thoughts, Annette at least I don't mix and party like you do, I show a very good example of what good citizens black people can be in this country. Annette, if you want to go to these meetin's you *go*, I don't want to fight those crazy people, let the police do it! What you think the police are here for? Let the police do it!! If you fight, they will arrest you!!

Annette!! Be sensible!! You can call me any name you want but I am not coming to your meeting! I do not like crowds!! I'm going to have a rest and read my Bible on my bed, and then at ten-thirty I am going to turn on the television and watch my show. Okay. Yes, yes, you can still come by tomorrow, we will go and look for the material. Yes, I wish you luck, of course!!

(SOUND: Knock on door.)

ELEANOR: *(Behind door.)* Velma?

VELMA: I go see you Annette. Yes, Eleanor.

(SOUND: Phone hangs up.)

ELEANOR: Mummy says I shouldn't bother you.

VELMA: No, it's alright. Come in.

(SOUND: Door opens.)

ELEANOR: *(Moving on.)* I just wanted to tell you ... that I think it's going to be alright.

VELMA: Oh well, thank you. How you know that?

ELEANOR: Because of my super ...

VELMA: Okay, well I'll believe you then. You are a nice child, have a chocolate, here.

ELEANOR: Thank you. I like these chocolates.

VELMA: I know you do.

ELEANOR: See, I think that the police will just ... catch them all and it will be over.

VELMA: Eleanor, the police ... don't like ... people that is not white.

ELEANOR: Why not?

VELMA: I don't know. I just know they always takes the side of the white. That is what I am told.

ELEANOR: Well it's not true. It's the worst lie I ever heard, 'cause Constable James? That came to our school in fire prevention week? He was really really really nice. He was the nicest man I met, and he was even nice to Saphira. And she's black.

VELMA: Alright, Elly, I believe you. Now go on off to bed, your Mummy will be angry with you.

ELEANOR: Velma, why is that picture of your brother on the floor?

VELMA: Because it fell, and I didn't pick it up.

Scene Ten

(Basement apartment.)

(SOUND: Presence of small group, cassette recorder clicked on.)

CARL: *(On tape.)* Okay, Pat, Dave, Gavin, Huntley—I come to you by tape for security reasons and that's the way it's gonna be till the end of the campaign—things are gettin' hairy, there's undercover everywhere, man, watch out for any guy that seems even more crazy than me, right? He's probably a cop, they always overdo it and and ... Enemies out there in ... big numbers, Communist scum fillin' the media with shit. There's Vietnamese gangs out there. Triads after us, man, and every black boy in town is packin' a piece. But the worst, the worst are the white liberals. So friggin' ungrateful, right? They don't even realize what we're doin' for their country, they're worse, man, they're even worse than than the wogs, right? When we take over, man, the hippies are the first to swing.

Scene Eleven

(Small living-room.)

KIMBERLY: *(At age 18. On phone to girlfriend.)* I'm the only one that gets to see Carl, nobody else gets to and he told me why, it's because he needs to have a lot of sex, because of the ... pressure, right? And that's fine with me, 'cause like, while he does it to me he talks, right? And he's made me feel much much better about the whole thing, like what he says is that it's like rats, right? Like, if you have rats in your house, you have to get rid of them. You feed them poison, you trap 'em, you kill 'em. Because they carry disease. Well Carl says that immigrant people are just like that, and I asked him, what about the nice ones, like I had two or three girlfriends in school that were immigrant kids, Mary and Elena, and he says, he says, "Kimmy, if you let three rats stay in your basement, then before you even turn around you got three hundred." And I can kind of see he's got a point.

Scene Ten *(continued)*

(Basement apartment.)

(SOUND: As before.)

CARL: *(On tape.)* I do have some ... victories to report to you. Fifty-two corner stores closed down, *every* taxi driver has a white face, *even* airport limousines, the subways and buses are white white white ...

Scene Twelve

(Bedroom.)

(SOUND: Rattle of newspaper.)

VELMA: *(Reading.)* Seventeen more non-whites murdered in six days. *(Internal.)* Satan is loose in the subways, he come from the deeps of the earth and he roamin' around in the bodies of young girls and boys. Stupid simple Velma. I thought somehow I was safe here, that Canada was like the sunny tip of a giant iceberg floatin' in a dark and bleedin' sea, but now it seems, the sea is risin'. My God in heaven will You forgive these servants of Satan? Or will they burn in everlastin' ...

Scene Thirteen

(Prison interview room.)

KIMBERLY: *(At age 31.)* I have no doubt whatsoever that I will go to hell. And I know exactly what it's gonna be like, too. What, this? Jail? No, jail is purgatory, waitin' it out, right? Just waitin', waitin', waitin' it out, all this time to think, and I don't ever think of nothin'. How can ya think with everybody's radio blarin'?

Scene Fourteen

(Classroom.)

(SOUND: Rustle, coughs of young pupils.)

ELEANOR: *(To her class.)* If the bad guys, the skinheads come in the house and start to kill Mummy and Daddy and Velma, I know what to do. I even practiced in the dark. Um, I, um, run out of my room, and then ... then I go down the stairs and—I try to open the front door and I try really hard and I get it, and then I run across the street even without shoes I run run run over to Katherine's house and I ring that doorbell over and over press as hard as I can and when Katherine's Mummy and Daddy come to the door I scream "Dial 911! Dial 911!" and then they do and the police will come and save Mummy and Daddy and Velma.

The only thing is, I wish I had a gun.

Without Contraries is no progression. Attraction and Repulsion. Reason and Energy, Love and Hate, are necessary to Human existance.

From these contraries spring what the religious call Good & Evil. Good is the passive that obeys Reason. Evil is the active springing from Energy.

Good is Heaven. Evil is Hell.

(Wm. Blake, "Marriage of Heaven and Hell")
c.1789

Scene Ten (continued)

(Basement apartment.)

(SOUND: As before.)

CARL: *(On tape. Very breathless, maybe drunk, stressed.)* No, what I'm saying is look out for the *organizers*, not the stupid dink in slippers, the brains, the ones that can talk to councils and cops and ... ministries ... who get the NDP scum workin' for 'em, do ya get me, do ya get what I'm sayin'? 'Cause you're not acting like you do—you're acting like a bunch of friggin' goofs beatin' up on little old ladies and black crackheads. *The brains.* We *got* to *get* to the *brains,* that's what they done in South Africa, it worked perfect, that's what they done in Nazi Germany Heil Heil, you kill the rooster and then the rest of 'em are just a bunch of chickens runnin' around with their heads cut off!! Find the brains, or this campaign is finished, gentlemen, and this commander is going to pour a large can of gasoline over myself and my woman, take a taxi over to Immigration, and right on the steps, right on the steps of our country's ...

Scene Fifteen

(Entrance hall of house.)

(SOUND: Door opens.)

ELEANOR: Velma! Velma! What did they say? Did they say yes? You can stay?

VELMA: For goodness sakes let me get my coat off, child!

ELEANOR: Oh please? Please tell me?

VELMA: It is none of your business, Eleanor. You are a child. And I don't have to tell you anything. *(Moving off.)*

(SOUND: VELMA runs up the wooden stairs.)

ELEANOR: *(Gasps in surprise.)* Velma!

Scene Sixteen

(Bedroom.)

(MUSIC: Ominous; continues underneath.)

(SOUND: Sheets rustle, mattress creaks, cat meows. CARL wakes up with a scream. He screams over and over.)

KIMBERLY: *(At age 18.)* Hey, Carl, it's okay! Baby baby. It's okay! It's me, Kimmy, we're here in our apartment, the cat's on the bed, everything's fine. Baby, oh baby.

CARL: It was ... sittin' on my chest. They had it ... sittin' on my chest, breathin' right in my face ...

KIMBERLY: Some kind of monster?

CARL: Get me a scotch, a glass of scotch.

KIMBERLY: *(Moving off.)* Okay scotch ... scotch, should I call someone Carl, Carl?

CARL: It's my generals, they're, they're ... conspiring an ... overthrow, that friggin' Danny he's never liked me, always always at the beginning you know when we were hangin' out he'd try to lose me, down the Eaton Centre and that, he'd try to get the other guys to lose me. They got their knives out, the knives are out, the knives are out ...

KIMBERLY: *(Moving on.)* No, no, no, baby, they love you, come here, it's okay, it's okay. I'm here, Kimmy's here.

CARL: No, man, I can't take it no more. I'm the only one with ideals around here, the rest of you, you don't really give a shit, you don't care, you don't care, you think I'm garbage, you think I'm nothing but a piece of garbage—

KIMBERLY: Oh, Carl no no. I love you so much, you know how much I love you ...

CARL: Do you? Do you?

(MUSIC: Ends.)

Scene Seventeen

(Eleanor's bedroom.)

ELEANOR: *(Crying.)*

(SOUND: Knock on door. Door opens.)

VELMA: Eleanor? *(Moving on.)* Don't say anything, just please, let me talk. I apologize for bein' harsh with you, I didn't mean to be hurtin' your feelin's. You is a very good child and you.... See, Eleanor, I always thought my eye beatin' and that picture fallin' meant I was to be deported. Now that I am landed, I am scared. What that picture fall for?

Scene Eighteen

(Prison interview room.)

KIMBERLY: *(At age 31.)* See, I had to prove to him that I cared. This was my *man*, can you understand that or are you one of those feminist dog dykes or something? Can you understand, when your man is like ... falling apart, you will do anything, like *anything* ... *(Near tears.)*

Scene Nineteen

(Bedroom.)

(MUSIC: Religious hymn on radio; continues underneath.)

VELMA: *(Internal.)* Velma, the only way to understand what is happenin' is to carefully go through what exactly happened last time the picture fell, and to see ... if ... it has any ... meanin' to what is happenin' now. Yes, and don't get upset, because then your mind will run off the track, okay, let us begin.

Scene Twenty

(Stairwell of abandoned building.)

(SOUND: Presence of small group.)

CARL: Face to face, I had to see youse face to face just so youse know how Carl deals with mut–iny. First off, I wipe off the blood, and second off, I put a knife through Danny's heart.

Scene Nineteen (continued)

(Bedroom.)

(MUSIC: As before.)

VELMA: *(Internal.)* The picture fall down in the mornin', and by afternoon I get a call from California to come now, Michael is very sick. Sara Dixon give me the money and I arrive there eight o'clock that evenin'.

Scene Twenty (continued)

(Stairwell of abandoned building.)

CARL: Danny didn't have no children, no nothin'. He didn't leave nothin' but a half-drunk glass of Remy Martin. Which I threw in his face.

Scene Nineteen (continued)

(Bedroom.)
(MUSIC: As before.)
VELMA: *(Internal.)* It very hot in Los Angeles, like walkin' through syrup. William, his ... flat mate was there to pick me up. When I shook his hand it was too soft, and wet.

Scene Eighteen (continued)

(Prison interview room.)
(SOUND: Conversation, steel doors in background.)
KIMBERLY: *(At age 31.)* He was so good to me, like in bed, right? Like he was the only guy who—like to other guys a woman was just a drumstick, right? But Carl, man, I didn't know in my life that anything could feel that good like ya know on Star Trek when they want to go somewhere and they're like ... dissolved ...

Scene Nineteen (continued)

(Bedroom.)
(MUSIC: As before.)
VELMA: *(Internal.)* Michael's apartment was leather and silver, two things Michael always have loved, and he was doin' well, too, had a very good job with the government, was always sending us lots of money, all the family, especially at Christmas, when he couldn't make it back to see us, all the leather, three leather couches, leather lazy boy chair in front of the biggest television, zebra rug, real sterling silver shinin' everywhere and I could not see Michael. I say but where is Michael and William point ... and there you were so thin, so black you look part of the couch like a fold, I was thinkin', in the couch ...

Scene Twenty (continued)

(Stairwell of abandoned building.)
CARL: A ceremony this night, a candlelight ceremony to honour the dead ... they will walk arm in arm some five six hundred strong

across the dark park to the pond, see, and they're gonna be lighting their candles at the very moment that dusk becomes dark ...

Scene Eighteen (continued)

(Prison interview room.)
KIMBERLY: *(At age 31.)* And I'm thinkin' yeah, that's what you do to me, Carl, in bed, I'm like dusk turning to dark ...

Scene Nineteen (continued)

(Bedroom.)
(MUSIC: As before.)
VELMA: *(Internal.)* And I look in that William's eye and I see poison. I see that he have wanted Michael to own, and that is why Michael never come to us at Christmas, I see that he have fight with Michael every time Michael have any kind of friend, that he have screamed and yelled at Michael on the street, saying he lookin' at girls, and boys, other people. This boy, this William had wanted Michael for a pet. He had poison in him eye.

Scene Twenty (continued)

(Stairwell of abandoned building.)
CARL: And ... I think, let's just see if we can't go and see if we can't turn that candlelight into ... conflagration!!
(SOUND: The generals' war cry.)

Scene Nineteen (continued)

(Bedroom.)
(MUSIC: As before.)
VELMA: *(Internal.)* And I turn around and I well beat him up, and he yellin' and screamin' at me, "You wicked woman, you wicked wicked woman," but I don't care, I fightin' for my brother's life.

Scene Eighteen (continued)

(Prison interview room.)
KIMBERLY: *(At age 31.)* Like, it's just that we didn't know how we

were supposed to tell who were the brains, like, Carl always expected us to guess half of what he wanted, right? So I remembered him one time sayin' somethin' about how he hated people that wore buttons, right? Like first on his list was abortion buttons, right, 'cause Carl really loved babies and he figured these bitches were just like murdering baby Canadians, and then any of that Communist stuff like "Save the Whales," or "Stop Violence Against Women" or anything like that. So while he's in the bathroom I pass this on to the others, right?

Scene Twenty-One

(Bedroom.)

(SOUND: Clothes rustle.)

ELEANOR: Where are you going this time, Velma?

VELMA: Just to a service.

ELEANOR: What does that button say?

VELMA: It say "Lord is God," Eleanor. I tole you that many time.

ELEANOR: I know, I just like it when you say it.

VELMA: You talk too smart sometimes, young lady. Now goodnight.

ELEANOR: Velma? When you come and kiss me goodnight? My eyes will be closed but I won't be asleep!!

VELMA: Goodnight!

Scene Eighteen (continued)

(Prison interview room.)

KIMBERLY: *(At age 31.)* What can I tell ya? I guess I just ... went I ... turned into ... like a Vietnam guy in a village or some crap like I ... went like the top of my head's comin' off and a windstorm is pipin' through like a movie, like I don't know have you ever killed a mouse? Like—had one of those sticky traps and it's squealin' and you like hit it on the head with a hammer or something? You just do it 'cause you have to do it? Well I hadn't done nothin' yet, see? And Carl, I think ... he was lookin' ... at Darlene ... I mean ... I know he was, and like, I had to prove to him, that I.... So I don't know, I just picked any nigger with a button ...

(SOUND: VELMA begins to sing "Mango"; continues underneath.)

I take fourteen different kinds of medication for this. And my arm here, it don't stop movin' like this, see this? Anytime, even while I sleep, don't ask me why. And I got like a priest in my mind or somethin', every time I sit down to pee or lie down to sleep he's in there, forcin' my memory to play it again. I don't throw up any more, but it does put me in a really bad mood. I don't mind so much remembering what she looked like as the expression in her eyes. *That is wearin' me down, right?* Like the way water does a rock? You ever seen that? Wear it right down to sand, man, right down to white sand.

Scene Twenty-Two

(Park; a candlelight ceremony.)

(SOUND: Large crowd singing "We Shall Overcome," softly, surely.)

VELMA: *(Internal. As she approaches the crowd.)* And I see tall angels on either side of Michael, reach down they brown hands and pull from his sweet head his ... Michaelfruit, the ruby juice running down his white sheets then his fruit explode! Circlin', sparkin', powerin' those black angels up through the hospital ceiling leavin' only a crack in the—

(SOUND: Suddenly the singing is harshly interrupted by violence. People are screaming, there is pandemonium.)

Scene Eighteen (continued)

(Prison interview room.)

KIMBERLY: *(At age 31.)* When I get out? I'll get a little place in Kingston so I can visit Carl on a regular basis.

Scene Twenty-Three

(Bedroom.)

ELEANOR: *(Internal.)* I don't ever sleep at night Velma, so honest, you can come and hold my hand any middle of the night, I even make my Daddy keep the window open just a little even on the winterest nights, 'cause I know that ghosts are like the steam from the kettle, that's what you told me once, and they can fit through the smallest ...

Scene Twenty-Four

(Park.)

(SOUND: Screaming. Violence continues. VELMA is attacked by KIMBERLY, becomes slow motion; continues underneath.)

VELMA: *(Internal.)* Oohh, white woman, Satan have made spit-balls with your soul, I see him laughin' through your eyeballs. I hope ... that one day you will gather ...

(MUSIC: Creeps in, builds to a climax.)

Michael! Michael! Hey tell me something Michael, did that William, your flat mate, did he get your furniture after you died? I seen the way he looked at your leather and all the sterling silver ... *(She laughs joyously.)*

(MUSIC: Ends.)

Scene Twenty-Five

(Bedroom.)

ELEANOR: *(Sings.)* Mango mango mango vey, mango teen, mango do do's, soo-tey ma-tan; tey tey bo ... all for me ... mango mango ... mango vey mango teen ... *(Fades underneath.)*

CARL: *(Over singing. A voice in Kimberly's memory.)* I'll get out, I'll get outta here Kimmy, and then, then, I'm gonna wage war, that, that was just foolin' around.

(VELMA joins ELEANOR singing "Mango.")

(MUSIC: Ominous music begins underneath, then up and out as ELEANOR laughs.)

Te Pouaka Karaehe:
The Glass Box

by Renée

When asked to describe herself for a new audience, RENÉE, who uses only her first name for her writing, refers to a recent talk with a group of women about their own labels, in which each woman easily came up with dozens. "There are all sorts of labels, a real mixture," she says. "I'm a writer, a lesbian, a feminist, a mother, an older woman, working class, divorced, a fanatical gardener ..." The list goes on. Although "writer" is at the top of her heap, it was one she only added in the last decade. Renée began writing plays at the age of fifty, and in ten years has become one of New Zealand's most successful and highly regarded stage writers. Since 1981, she has had a dozen plays produced, and has had a novel and a collection of short stories published.

Renée also learned about her Maori heritage, her mother's people, late in life. Her mother lived in a society where it was shameful to be a Maori, and simply never talked about it. "I think knowledge of my mother's people has been a rather interesting if sometimes painful journey to make," Renée says, reflecting on the fact that *Te Pouaka Karaehe* is her first play based primarily on Maori lives. Renée says she has been reluctant to write Maori characters, but for this play drew on her own experiences of living in cities as a way into the story of a Maori woman's attempts to reconcile two worlds.

"One of the reasons I haven't written a work where Maoris are the main protagonists is because I don't have the background of a *marae*,' says Renée. "But I do have a lot of background in small towns and the city, and I think that those are the sorts of people that I will write about. Brought up in a European tradition, Renée left school at the age of twelve, and earned her university degree, mainly by correspondence, when she was thirty-eight. She describes her education as formed mainly by English and American literary sources. Only recently have such writers as Patricia Grace and Witi Ihimaera emerged to add strong Maori voices to New Zealand's literary landscape.

"As I get a bit older, and I've read a lot and thought a lot, I realize that my experience is as valid as anyone else's. My experience of being—this is not very nice—but sometimes I'm too light [skinned] for some and too dark for others," says Renée. "It's from that point of view that I'll probably write a lot more [Maori characters]. I do acknowledge my father's people as well, and I wouldn't by any means turn my back on that."

Renée says she has written about the conflict between city and country values and pursuits in earlier work, and continues to be interested in how rural people reconcile themselves to an urban lifestyle. For Maoris in particular, such a shift can mean weakening ties that hold them to their people, as well as to the land. "I like to think about the effect of the city on people, not only Maori people but *Pakeha* people as well," says Renée. "I also believe that we need lots and lots more Maori people, particularly women, in powerful positions and that comes at a huge cost to those women."

In this radio play, Renée uses the catalyst of the *tangi* (funeral) of a Maori elder to illustrate the workings of these issues of cultural assimilation or rejection. Two of her other plays are also based on deaths, including *Wednesday to Come*, a play about a working-class family whose father kills himself during the Depression. (Renée's father committed suicide when she was a young child, although she points out that *Wednesday to Come* is not an autobiographical play.) "Deaths always bring lots of things to the surface," says Renée. "I think they're a time when you reflect on the relationship you had with that person, especially if you resent part of the power that the other person had for whatever reason, that you let them have, I guess."

Te Pouaka Karaehe's story of one Maori woman, Elizabeth/Irihapeti, dramatizes Renée's thinking about the difficulties experienced by Maoris who achieve positions of power in a predominantly white society—even when their desire for power isn't personally motivated. Renée describes the suspicion encountered by people who have the opportunity to change their lives and hope to change the lives of others. She too has experienced such distrust: "I'm working class and some of my relatives feel, quite rightly, a little suspicious of my having a university degree. That suspicion is formed by various experiences they've no doubt had with people who have university degrees, teachers or bureaucrats or doctors or all those sorts of people who have lots of power. So when one of their number seems to join those people, they are a little suspicious—until they meet up with you or you visit them and they find out that you're just the same as you were."

Approached to write a drama for a Canadian audience, Renée says she felt this theme would resonate for both Native and non-Native listeners. "I thought of Canadian Indians, and maybe other ethnic minorities, but mainly Canadian Indians, who would perhaps know what it was like to work very hard to get into a position where you've got some power, where you can be a guide for your people, and realize at the same time that what you've done is set yourself up for them to feel as though they can't trust you any more, as though you've joined the enemy. I also thought the scenario wasn't far removed from *Pakeha* people's minds," she says.

Te Pouaka Karaehe: The Glass Box is Renée's first original play for radio, though she has adapted two of her stage plays and has had short stories read on air. Renée, who says she generally leans toward a naturalistic structure on stage, uses a realistic style broken by thoughts or music in this play, a kind of "naturalism with interruptions." What most interests her about radio is the possibility for innovative use of sound, although she points out that with this drama she was most interested in following an argument in her own mind.

"The medium is a hearing medium, there's lots and lots of scope in it. You're free to go anywhere and do anything as long as you use sound to convey it. I don't think my play goes anywhere near the kind of scope that you can use on radio. The internal reflection and the external conversation or flashbacks I've used are only a few of the things that one can use," Renée says, adding that this experience has made her eager to write more radio drama.

In the end, Elizabeth does accept her grandmother's vision and reconciles herself to working for change in the city. "There's the sense that somebody has to be there, that the world is not going to stand still," says Renée. "Maoris, both young and old, will want and need guides in the city. Just as her sister takes up the responsibility of guiding people around

Takitimu, Elizabeth takes up, albeit reluctantly, the job of guiding people through the maze, through the glass box of the city.

"Sometimes you can spend quite a lot of time resenting things and they can be resolved quite quickly, perhaps by coming face to face with death or just having time to think away from where you live and where you work. Elizabeth has one of those sorts of moments."

RENÉE was born in Napier, New Zealand in 1929, of Ngati Kahungunu (Maori) and Scottish ancestry. She is one of the most highly regarded playwrights in her country; her themes are serious, her tone frequently comic and her politics radically feminist. Before beginning to write for the theatre in her fifties, she raised three sons and worked at a number of jobs, including English and drama teaching. She also published short stories and directed a number of amateur stage productions. Her first stage play, the 1981 *Setting the Table*, was a feminist debate about women using the same means of violence as men. *Secrets* (1981) encompasses three short plays with two women characters. Her 1982 revue, *What Did You Do in the War Mummy?*, was toured by the feminist collective magazine *Broadsheet* to celebrate its tenth anniversary. *Groundwork* (1983) is about the Springbok rugby tour of New Zealand two years earlier, and *Asking for It*, also written in 1983, is a popular comedy revue about the three Rs: religion, rape and racism. *Wednesday to Come* (1984), *Pass It On* (1986) and *Jeannie Once* (1990) form a critically acclaimed trilogy of plays about four generations of women in a working-class family, set in the Depression, the 1951 waterfront lockout and the late nineteenth century. In 1990 she staged two other new plays, *Touch of the Sun*, about two women confronting a death, and *Form*, a commissioned play for schools. Her most recent play, *Missionary Position* (1991) is about "who's on top and who's on bottom and how they feel about it." Her works in fiction are *Finding Ruth* (1987), a book of short stories, and the novel *Willy Nilly* (1990). She has adapted two of her stage plays for radio. She lives in Dunedin, New Zealand.

Characters

ELIZABETH Maori civil servant, mid thirties
NANNY Elizabeth's grandmother, elderly
TAMATI TV journalist, late thirties
WIKI Elizabeth's sister, early thirties
AUNTIE SARAH mid seventies
JOURNALISTS ONE, TWO, THREE

Production Credits

Te Pouaka Karaehe: The Glass Box was commissioned by the Canadian Broadcasting Corporation for Morningside Drama and first broadcast on the CBC Radio network on May 15, 1991.

ELIZABETH Nicki Guadagni
NANNY Joyce Campion
TAMATI Damon Redfern
WIKI Jacquiline Samuda
AUNTIE SARAH Jill Frappier
JOURNALISTS Bryan Foster, Brian Pearcy

Produced and directed in Toronto by Gregory J. Sinclair. Casting Consultant: Linda Grearson. Language Advisors: Michael Hallowes and Robin Nightingale. Recording Engineer: Glen McLaughlin. Sound effects by John Stewart. Production Assistant: Kate Nickerson. Script Editor: Dave Carley. Executive Producer of Morningside Drama: James Roy.

[Note: A glossary of Maori terms appears on page 50.]

Te Pouaka Karaehe:
The Glass Box

Scene One

(Elizabeth's apartment, Wellington.)

(MUSIC: Waiata, a Maori song; fades underneath.)

(SOUND: ELIZABETH is packing; rustle of clothing, sound of clothes hangers in cupboard.)

ELIZABETH: *(Internal.)* The waiata won't go away. Every time I stop working, walking, wondering, worrying, there it is. Even now, packing to go and see her for the last time, it won't let up. It's Nanny, of course. Maybe she's heard the rumours about my job? It all depends, Nanny, on whether they see my job as a political appointment or not. You know what new governments are like. But it doesn't look good. Now, shall I take my lined jacket or not? Takitimu can be cold in October.

(SOUND: Clothes in cupboard, hangers.)

(MUSIC: Waiata comes up, fades out.)

NANNY: *(Reverb.)* Irihapeti. Irihapeti come home to Takitimu. You must return to Takitimu.

ELIZABETH: Go away, Nanny, go away! I'm packing, isn't that enough? There's a meeting with the minister to get through, a briefing she'll ignore. There's gossip I need to hear, people I have to lobby. I had that funny dream again last night and I bet that sister of mine will ring again. I say to her "Wiki I'll be there!" but no, she has to ring!

NANNY: *(Reverb.)* You must tangi over me, Irihapeti. I'm setting out on the journey to the meeting place where our tupuna wait. You must farewell me so I can go with a clear heart.

ELIZABETH: *(Irritated.)* I'm coming, Nanny, I'm coming!

Scene Two

(Outside Wellington Airport.)

(SOUND: ELIZABETH's footsteps, hurrying into the airport.)

ELIZABETH: *(Internal.)* There's just a chance I'll escape those vultures!

(SOUND: A bunch of journalists mixing with airport ambience. Airport background noise continues through scene.)

(Internal.) Damn, damn, damn!

JOURNALIST ONE: Miss Hema!

JOURNALIST TWO: Will you get out of my way, you fool! Miss Hema!

ELIZABETH: *(Internal.)* Oh well, into the old razzle dazzle.

JOURNALIST THREE: Just a second of your time, Miss Hema!

ELIZABETH: *(Internal.)* I suppose their mothers love them. *(Aloud, authoritatively, with great charm.)* Good morning everyone! I'm in a terrible hurry I'm afraid!

(SOUND: Babble of protest: "Please, Miss Hema." "This way, Miss Hema." "What did the minister say, Miss Hema?" "What are your plans, Miss Hema?" etc.)

(Internal.) This must be how Daniel felt when he was shoved into the lion's den.

JOURNALIST ONE: Just a quick word, Miss Hema!

JOURNALIST THREE: Is it true the incoming government has plans to reorganize the Financial Advisory Group and your job will be on the line?

JOURNALIST TWO: How did you feel when you heard that Nanny Marama had died, Miss Hema?

ELIZABETH: *(Internal. Sarcastic.)* I danced for joy, you fool, what else? Do you think I'd tell you I cried all night?

JOURNALIST TWO: Will the media be allowed at the tangi, Miss Hema?

JOURNALIST THREE: You're the first Maori woman to be appointed to such a post. Is all this speculation and rumour simply a matter of prejudice?

ELIZABETH: *(Internal. Sarcastic.)* Even an intellectual silkworm like you should know the answer to that! *(Aloud.)* That's a very interesting question. Perhaps you should ask those who make it their business to speculate.

JOURNALIST TWO: Exactly what was your relationship to Nanny Marama, Miss Hema?

ELIZABETH: *(Internal.)* She was the puppet-mistress and I was the puppet. Most of the time I hated her guts. *(Aloud.)* She was my grandmother.

JOURNALIST ONE: There's been some criticism of your leadership of the Financial Advisory Group. Are you being consulted about the rumoured changes?

JOURNALIST THREE: What's your reaction to these persistent rumours, Miss Hema?

ELIZABETH: I make it a rule to ignore rumours.

(SOUND: A confused babble of journalists all speaking at once: "What about this morning's meeting?" "Is it true the minister requested your resignation?" "How long will you be away from Wellington?" "Miss Hema!" "Miss Hema!" "Miss Hema!" etc.)

TAMATI: *(Moving on. Under babble.)* Kia ora Irihapeti.

ELIZABETH: *(Angry.)* What the hell are you doing here!

TAMATI: Nice to see you, too. Okay everyone! Miss Hema is mine.

JOURNALIST ONE: Come off it, Tama! Give us a break!

JOURNALIST TWO: You can't just swipe her from under our noses!

ELIZABETH: *(Irritated.)* Nobody's swiping anyone! I'm going to my grandmother's funeral and in my opinion this isn't the time for you to be badgering me!

(SOUND: Journalists' voices rise in protest: "Come on, Miss Hema." "Give us a break!" "Just a short statement!" etc.)

TAMATI: *(In an undertone.)* They won't give up. You have to talk to someone. It might as well be me.

ELIZABETH: My office will be releasing a press statement early next week.

JOURNALIST ONE: You were one of the organizers of the Land March which the new government criticized when they were in opposition. Do you think this has a bearing on the present situation?

ELIZABETH: I don't know what you mean by "present situation."

JOURNALIST TWO: Nanny Marama was a very well-known guide in the Takitimu area. Did she say who would carry on her work?

ELIZABETH: *(Internal.)* You made it very clear years ago, didn't you, Nanny. *(Aloud.)* Yes she did. My sister, Wiki.

JOURNALIST TWO: Will you challenge that decision?

ELIZABETH: Of course not!

TAMATI: *(Undertone.)* Quickly, Irihapeti, you choose. Them or me.

(SOUND: Babble of importuning voices yelling, "Please, Miss Hema." "Just a couple of words!" "Nanny Marama!")

ELIZABETH: All right, Tamati! All right!

TAMATI: This way, Miss Hema. Sorry everyone! My trick! *(Moving off.)*

(SOUND: Babble of angry and disappointed voices fade as ELIZABETH and TAMATI leave the reporters behind and walk through the airport lounge.)

Scene Three

(Airport, private room.)

TAMATI: It's times like these I wonder why I'm in the trade. You should be okay in here.

ELIZABETH: You almost sound as though you care!

TAMATI: Now, Irihapeti, is that kind?

ELIZABETH: I stopped being kind a long time ago. And you didn't get your own TV show by being a sweet and tender pussy-cat.

AIRPORT ANNOUNCER: Air NZ Flight 423 to Napier is boarding at gate six. Air NZ flight to Napier is boarding at gate six.

TAMATI: I'm sorry about Nanny Marama. Takitimu won't be the same without her.

ELIZABETH: Look, I have to check my tickets. If you must go on with this charade I'd be obliged if you'd hurry it up!

TAMATI: This is your first visit back to Takitimu since you were made Director of the Financial Advisory Group, isn't it?

ELIZABETH: I've been busy.

TAMATI: Nanny was very proud of you, Irihapeti.

ELIZABETH: Of course she was. I was her creation. She wound me up and I did everything just the way she wanted.

TAMATI: You've always refused to be interviewed by me.

ELIZABETH: Don't play games, Tama. Once upon a time we were lovers who swore to love each other forever. I spoiled that fairy tale. I ran away. Your requests for interviews were rather blatant attempts to reopen old wounds.

TAMATI: At first perhaps.

ELIZABETH: I don't trust any journalists, especially those who work for TV.

TAMATI: Is this the right time to be scoring points?

ELIZABETH: You make it irresistible, Tamati. And you're not exactly renowned for altruism.

TAMATI: Believe it or not I was doing my St. George bit. I'm interested in the gossip about the possible axing of your job but I don't want to nag you about it now.

ELIZABETH: *(Disbelievingly.)* Nice one, Tama.

TAMATI: Look, Nanny Marama's dead. Surely you can forget our differences for the moment?

AIRPORT ANNOUNCER: Air NZ flight 423 to Napier boarding at gate six. All passengers aboard please.

ELIZABETH: Tamati March does nothing for nothing.

AIRPORT ANNOUNCER: Last call for passengers boarding Air NZ flight 423 to Napier. Your flight is boarding through gate six.

ELIZABETH: I have to go.

TAMATI: Me too.

ELIZABETH: Are you playing games or what?

TAMATI: You don't think I'd miss Nanny's tangi, do you?

ELIZABETH: Now who's scoring points!

(SOUND/MUSIC: Airport noise as door opens onto main lounge. Waiata fades in over airport noise, then merges with interior sound of 747 plane.)

Scene Four

(Inside plane.)

(SOUND: Plane interior, people chatting.)

TAMATI: You okay, Irihapeti?

ELIZABETH: You're joking! And stop using that name!

TAMATI: Is Wiki meeting you at Napier?

ELIZABETH: Auntie Sarah will see to that. She clings to this weird idea that because Wiki and I are sisters we need to be together.

TAMATI: And Wiki will take over Nanny Marama's role? I can't say I'm surprised.

ELIZABETH: It's all arranged. Nanny saw to that. I bet at this very moment my sister's awash in a sea of memories and smug satisfactions. You'd think marriage and a baby would've cured her of being the romantic kid she started out as, but she's just the same. And why not? All her dreams came true. She's the one who'll pass on the history and guide the people around the ancient places of Takitimu. When my sister's old she'll be Nanny Wiki, and I, maybe I'll be the retired Director of the Financial Advisory Group reporting to the minister and maybe I won't!

(MUSIC: Waiata fades in and merges with:)

Scene Five

(Car interior.)

(SOUND: A small modern car on a tar-sealed road. A baby's half-hearted cries continue intermittently.)

WIKI: Hush Bubbie, there's a good girl. I couldn't refuse Auntie Sarah, much as I wanted to. At least when we're in the car we can't be nagged into ringing Irihapeti all the time! That Auntie Sarah's a real worry-wart! "Maybe she'll change her mind. Maybe she'll miss the plane." So silly. If my big-time sister doesn't want to drop all those very important things she's always in the middle of, then it's her that misses out, eh Bubs.

(SOUND: Baby's clucking.)

Good girl. See, your Auntie Irihapeti pretends not to care about life in the city, the high-powered career, the perks, the flash apartment, but place it all in jeopardy and she starts scrambling and clawing like all the rest. I've seen her nose wrinkle when she looks at our house. "Just your three-bedroom, kitchen and living-room Maori Affairs ordinary," I can hear her thinking. But we like it, don't we, Bubbie. My sister. You wouldn't believe how much she's changed. Oh yes. Once upon a time, Bubbie, my sister Irihapeti went away for good and Ms Elizabeth Hema came back. And that was that.

(SOUND: Baby's clucking turns to crying.)

Bored huh? Can't say I blame you. Hang on Bubbie, won't be long now.

(MUSIC: Waiata fades to:)

Scene Six

(Inside plane.)

(SOUND: Plane interior, as before.)

TAMATI: Are you okay, Elizabeth?

ELIZABETH: You've asked me that stupid question before! Just give it a rest will you? ... Oh damn! ... Sorry. Just because my life's hoha there's no need to take it out on you.

TAMATI: It's okay.

ELIZABETH: Is it?

TAMATI: We've said worse things to each other. Just lean back and rest.

(MUSIC: Waiata fades in, then out.)

ELIZABETH: *(Internal.)* Oh yes, we scratched and seared each other with words, once. But now we're older and the city's laid its smart hands on us. From the outside we're the ones who made-our-mark-and-loved-every-minute and that's partly true. But for me, it's not turning out the way it was meant. I wonder if Nanny realizes her cherished plan has gone sour.

(MUSIC: Waiata fades in, continues underneath the following.)

Scene Seven

(Internal memory. A younger ELIZABETH and NANNY.)

NANNY: So there you are, Irihapeti! Why you always look like a dying duck in a thunderstorm, eh? Still holding that anger inside because we sent you away?

ELIZABETH: I'm fine, Nanny.

NANNY: Are you? You enjoy your work?

ELIZABETH: I enjoy my work.

NANNY: Irihapeti, your Nanny has a favour to ask. Will you talk to Meri Ropata? She won't listen to me. Says her mind's made up. She's off to her cousin's and she can't wait to scrape Takitimu from her shoes!

ELIZABETH: Oh Nanny, not the big rah-rah speech please! In any case Meri wouldn't take any notice of anything I said!

NANNY: The city's no place for her.

ELIZABETH: Times have changed, Nanny.

NANNY: But not people!

ELIZABETH: Ask Wiki.

NANNY: Your sister doesn't know the city.

ELIZABETH: I thought Wiki knew everything.

NANNY: There's trouble between you two?

ELIZABETH: There's no trouble.

NANNY: I might be old but I'm not senile.

ELIZABETH: You should be warming yourself in the sun with Auntie Sarah and the other old ones, and letting us young ones get on with it. If we make mistakes, then they're our mistakes, not ones you made for us!

NANNY: I only had two mokopuna, two grandchildren, and I had to do the best I could, for you and Wiki and for our people. I wanted you in the city so we have someone there when we need help.

ELIZABETH: Noone comes to me for help. They think I've stopped protesting and all they remember is that I got myself a fancy university degree and eventually a job where every day I'm mixing it with politicians and big business. They're convinced I've turned myself into a brown Pakeha, an Auntie Tom, and they wouldn't come near me with a forty-foot pole!

NANNY: They'll learn. Give them time. They're not used to having an ear in high finance.

ELIZABETH: And those I work with are not all that sure of me, either. It can get very lonely, Nanny.

NANNY: What happened to that Tamati Marsh you were so keen on?

ELIZABETH: He's got his own show.

NANNY: No need to tell me what I already know girl! I got a TV! What happened between you and him?

(MUSIC: Waiata fades.)

Scene Eight

(Inside Napier airport.)

(SOUND: Airport ambience, baby sounds.)

WIKI: There you are, Bubbie. You've been fed and changed and you're all prettied up to say hello to your Auntie Irihapeti. Make sure you smile now.

(SOUND: Airport sound swells, then fades.)

Kia ora Irihapeti. I'm pleased you came.

ELIZABETH: *(Moving on.)* Kia ora Wiki. Why wouldn't I come?

TAMATI: Good to see you, Wiki. And who's this?

WIKI: Huia. Although everyone calls her Bubbie. I had to bring her. I'm still feeding her myself. Here Bubbie, say kia ora to your Auntie.

ELIZABETH: Kia ora Huia. Come to your Auntie.

(SOUND: Baby clucking. Airport noise left behind as they move to the carpark; sliding door, traffic.)

TAMATI: She's smiling at you.

ELIZABETH: It's probably wind.

WIKI: The car's over here. Auntie Sarah'll be chuffed to see you, Tama.

(SOUND/MUSIC: Waiata begins, fades underneath car pulling up on gravel road.)

Scene Nine

(Outside Auntie Sarah's house.)

(MUSIC: Waiata swells, then fades.)

AUNTIE SARAH: *(Moving on. Near tears.)* Where is she? Where is my darling girl? Irihapeti, Irihapeti! My arms are empty, so empty! Come to Auntie, darling, you must fill that empty space. *(Hugging and kissing.)* Oh Irihapeti, how will I manage without that bossy sister of mine!

ELIZABETH: I'm sorry, Auntie Sarah.

AUNTIE SARAH: One day you will know how I feel. One of you will leave the other. One day.

TAMATI: Kia ora Auntie Sarah.

AUNTIE SARAH: Kia ora Tamati. *(Hugging and kissing him.)* Come in my darlings, come in! You must have some tea and then I'll take you to see Nanny. What a nice boy you are, Tamati, coming to see an old Auntie at this time.

(SOUND/MUSIC: Footsteps up wooden stairs sound through waiata.)

TAMATI: I'm glad I could be here, Auntie.

AUNTIE SARAH: Where's my Bubbie? Come to your Auntie Sarah.

Scene Ten

(Auntie Sarah's kitchen.)

(SOUND: Tea being poured. Cups and saucers placed on tray.)

WIKI: I'm sorry about your job, Irihapeti. Is it true you'll lose it?

ELIZABETH: Maybe I'll come home and stay home.

WIKI: Your home is in the city!

ELIZABETH: This is my turangawaewae, my place to stand, and no smart apartment in the city can alter that!

WIKI: Settle down! All I meant was you're a city person now.

ELIZABETH: I have this weird dream and it keeps coming back. I'm a little girl again and I'm inside a glass box crying to get out and I can't get anyone to hear me.

(SOUND: Baby's cry.)

TAMATI: *(Approaching.)* Bubbie needs you, Wiki.

WIKI: Oh Irihapeti, that's awful.

(SOUND: Baby's cry swells.)

(Calling.) All right Bubbie! Tamati, you talk to my sister. *(Leaving.)* Glass box. Sounds awful!

ELIZABETH: My family have never quite grasped that you and I are past tense.

TAMATI: I haven't forgotten you once said you loved me.

ELIZABETH: No sense singing old songs, Tama. I had to do what Nanny mapped out for me.

TAMATI: She didn't say you couldn't have a life of your own!

ELIZABETH: No, you did! You wanted a wife who'd put you first!

TAMATI: I remember being so angry with that old woman. Who did she think she was? Trying to run your life! Oh I was very righteous about it.

ELIZABETH: Yes. You thought running my life was your prerogative. Once I'd made the tea and written the leaflets, of course.

TAMATI: Took me a while to see that.

ELIZABETH: It was crazy anyway. You wanted a wife and kids and Nanny wanted some sort of financial guru. Didn't matter what I wanted.

TAMATI: What did Wiki mean? Glass box.

ELIZABETH: Nothing important.

TAMATI: Who are you punishing, Irihapeti?

ELIZABETH: *(Upset but fighting it.)* The city sucks us in and we forget everything except the rise in salary and what comes with it.

TAMATI: Is that how you see yourself?

ELIZABETH: *(Bitter.)* Oh we might pay lip service when we go back at Christmas or for a tangi or a wedding but it's out of sight, out of mind! That's what they think, isn't it?

TAMATI: That's sick!

ELIZABETH: It sure as hell is!

TAMATI: Irihapeti, what happened this morning? With the Minister?

ELIZABETH: You might as well know, I suppose. She said my job was secure and you know what I said? I said I wasn't sure! Now there's a scoop for you!

(SOUND/MUSIC: Waiata fades in; footsteps sound through waiata. Waiata fades for the karanga, a Maori summons or lament. The karanga fades; continues faintly underneath.)

Scene Eleven

(Verandah of meeting house where the coffin lies.)

(SOUND: Outside ambience.)

AUNTIE SARAH: Here she is, Irihapeti, here is your Nanny.

ELIZABETH: Kia ora Nanny.

AUNTIE SARAH: My sister's spirit is waiting to fly to the place where the waters meet, where our tupuna are waiting to gather her in. Oh how will I bear this lonely time until I too am called to be with the old ones! Sit here, Irihapeti, and you too, Wiki, here we will wait for her spirit to reach Cape Reinga.

(SOUND: The karanga swells slowly, then fades to sounds of women seated round coffin: breathing, a cough, a sigh. Baby clucking.)

ELIZABETH: *(Internal.)* I wonder if you can see us, Nanny? All sitting solemnly round you. Is everything an open book now? Do you know about my job? Are you facing the possibility that I'll turn it down? Or will you refuse to accept that even in death?

WIKI: *(Aloud.)* It's funny to see Nanny so still. She was always so full of energy. You're very like her, Irihapeti.

ELIZABETH: If I thought that I'd probably get in and lie in the coffin beside her.

WIKI: You're educated, you're living in a different time and you spend most of your life in a different place, but you're her double.

ELIZABETH: So why did she choose you to fill her shoes?

WIKI: It wasn't my idea to put my feet in her prints, but what could I do?

ELIZABETH: She loved you best! She gave you Takitimu!

WIKI: I couldn't refuse her. I'll never forget her coming to get us after the accident.

(MUSIC: Waiata swells softly. Reverb.)

(SOUND: A child sobbing through music.)

Scene Twelve

(A memory.)

(SOUND: Bustle of NANNY's arrival.)

NANNY: Where are they? Where are my mokopuna? Nanny's here, my darlings! Nanny's here! *(Hugging.)* Nanny will look after you. Nanny's here. There, there, darlings! Nanny will take you home!

(MUSIC: Waiata swells, then fades.)

(Reverb.) Te Reinga is the place of departed spirits. When your Mummy and Daddy died, their spirits left their bodies and journeyed north to the Spirit's Leap. Just at the right moment an opening appears in the seaweeds, and their spirits take their final plunge into Te Reinga. On the last part of their journey they come to a river and drink of the water, then they cross over and are welcomed by name. Haeremai Rawiri! Haeremai Keri! That's what our tupuna will say. They'll have some kai waiting. If Mummy or Daddy refuse the food, their spirits are doomed to wander forever. So we must let them go, my darlings. Freely. We can't hold them back however much we might want to. We have to go on without them until we too make that journey.

(MUSIC: Waiata fades in from the memory to the present.)

Scene Thirteen

(Around Nanny's coffin on verandah.)

WIKI: She was sixty when she was landed with us. A lot of people would've said no.

ELIZABETH: Nanny liked to be in charge.

WIKI: She wanted the best for us.

ELIZABETH: And how did she know what was best, Wiki?

(MUSIC: The karanga fades in.)

AUNTIE SARAH: We must let her go, my darlings. Let her go. Oh my sister, don't look back at us grieving ones. Set your face to the sun and take your place among those who wait for you.

(MUSIC: Waiata fades in.)

Scene Fourteen

(At Auntie Sarah's. ELIZABETH has told them of her doubts.)

ELIZABETH: What will happen? They'll go to you with their worries, Wiki, like they always do and you'll sort it out.

AUNTIE SARAH: But who will your sister go to?

ELIZABETH: I've done all I can! The things Nanny set out for me to do have raised a barrier between me and the very people she said it would help! They're not interested in the ones who know how to play the games, how to work the system! They think we've sold out!

AUNTIE SARAH: She didn't ask any more of you than she asked of herself, my darling.

ELIZABETH: Nanny had no doubts about her role in Takitimu. She loved being the Queen Bee!

AUNTIE SARAH: When my sister married your grandfather he was a strong, vigorous young man. They planned on spending half their time in Takitimu and half in the city. She was mad keen to get a degree in commerce. Well, they got married and had a son, your father. Then your grandfather fell off his horse and boom went all the plans! She stayed in Takitimu, became his legs, and when it got worse, his mouthpiece. When he died it was too late. The threads that bound her to this place were too strong. The people wouldn't let her leave. She railed, got angry with them, but she stayed. Of course you want to know that what you're doing is appreciated but maybe, my darling, appreciation doesn't come with the package.

ELIZABETH: You're pushing me into that damned glass box and I'm there all on my own! Our people reach out to you! Why should I have anything less?

WIKI: Is that what you'll tell Bubbie when she grows up?

ELIZABETH: Nanny relived her ambitions through me. And she was so stubborn! "We have to have someone working through the system!" I can hear her now! But she didn't think of the cost! And I'm sure as hell sick of being the one who pays!

WIKI: Everything she did and everything she gave up thoughts of doing was for our people, never for herself.

ELIZABETH: Why should I live in the vague hope that someday Bubbie and kids like her will look through the glass and see someone like them looking back? Why the hell should I?

AUNTIE SARAH: Because you are Nanny's mokopuna and you are both guides. Wiki leads the people around Takitimu, reminds them of the old ways, encourages them in the language, tells them about our tupuna. You, Irihapeti, you will lead them through the maze of glass that is the city. You have to stay there. Otherwise they'll cut themselves when they stumble.

(MUSIC: Waiata fades in, then out.)

Scene Fifteen

(Airport.)

(SOUND: Airport ambience.)

ELIZABETH: So I'm here, Tamati. Nanny is too strong for me. Especially when she's backed up by Wiki and Auntie Sarah.

TAMATI: *(Lightly affectionate.)* Haere mai, Nanny Irihapeti, haere mai.

ELIZABETH: Wiki said I was like Nanny Marama but in her own way my sister's just as formidable.

(SOUND: Door opens onto airport noise. A group of journalists.)

JOURNALIST ONE: Here she is!

JOURNALIST TWO: Miss Hema!

JOURNALIST THREE: Miss Hema, rumours are persisting that there are government moves to replace you and other members of the Financial Advisory Group. Do you have any comment?

ELIZABETH: The Minister asked me to stay on and I said I'd think it over. I've done so and this morning I notified her of my acceptance.

(MUSIC: Waiata.)

(SOUND: Babble of comment underneath music, "Thanks, Miss Hema." "Great!" "Thanks very much!")

JOURNALIST TWO: How was the tangi, Miss Hema?

ELIZABETH: Nanny Marama is making her way to Te Reinga. She will not look back.

(SOUND: Airport noise takes over, then fades.)

TAMATI: What about dinner tonight?

ELIZABETH: Sorry, Tama, there's some people I have to see. But if I'm going to learn to live in a glass house I have to be very careful of people who throw stones, so I'll need all the friends I can get. Maybe tomorrow.

TAMATI: Tomorrow then.

ELIZABETH: Tama, do you really think I'm like Nanny Marama?

TAMATI: Doesn't really matter, does it? It'll be Nanny Irihapeti that Bubbie and her friends will rage at and fight with and hate and love. No glass box will stop them when they come looking.

ELIZABETH: Kia ora Tama.

TAMATI: Kia kaha Irihapeti.

(MUSIC: Waiata fades for end.)

Glossary of Maori terms

Cape Reinga: place of leaping, where departed spirits take their final leap
haere mai: welcome; come here
hoha: crazy
kai: food
karanga: summons; call
kia ora: greetings; be well
kia kaha: be strong
marae: meeting ground; village common
mokopuna: grandchild
Pakeha: European; white person
tupuna: ancestor
turangawaewae: place to stand; home
tangi: to cry; mourn
waiata: song

Venus Sucked In:
A Post-feminist Comedy

by Anne Chislett

For playwright ANNE CHISLETT, *Venus Sucked In: A Post-feminist Comedy* is a departure in several directions. It's her first play with all women characters, and only her second to take place in an urban setting. "When I started writing for Ontario as a Newfoundlander, I was in deep culture shock," says Chislett. "The early plays are observed. I'm not a farm girl. I used to have a list above my typewriter, 'beans, wheat, oats and barley,' because that's the order the crop came in. I'm getting better at looking at a field and knowing whether it's wheat or oats."

Although she has written mainly about rural characters, Chislett says that underlying her plays about the struggle between a Mennonite father and son or between a farm wife and her husband is a core that speaks to people of any gender or age, in any situation. "On the other hand, when you're writing in a voice that's a little closer to you, it's a lot easier," says Chislett. "It was less of a struggle to get inside the minds of women characters, but I have no real drive to write only about women."

Chislett describes *Venus Sucked In* as a "fairly light and satirical piece." The play explores the relationships between four female characters who have been in her thoughts for several years. She hopes to turn the stories of these women into a stage trilogy with the working title *Madder Music and More Wine*, drawn from Ernest Dowson's poem

"Cynara." "Speaking of a woman's frustration, it just seems to be a great reaction: stronger wine and madder music," says Chislett of the title. One plan for the stage version is to have all four involved with the same man, in a variety of relationships, not all sexual.

The women come from three different generations. *Venus Sucked In* includes a seventy-year-old woman who predates the recent wave of feminism and a seventeen-year-old who feels the movement is passé: Betty and her teenage granddaughter, Kathy. Kathy's mother, Liz, and her aunt, Bev, fit into the middle of the pendulum swinging between pre- and post-feminism. For the grandmother's character, Chislett found herself "watching the women of a generation beyond mine, women who essentially missed the opportunities and now know that they had the cleverness, the wit, the ability—everything but the opportunity. When they watch the next generation do what it wants, there is occasionally an edge."

Kathy, from the generation to come, is fed up with her mother's version of the feminist wars. Says Chislett: "The attitude is that the feminists are too loud, too strident. These kids don't have the problems, and they don't understand what the fuss is about." As signs of the changing times, Chislett refers to a recent spate of articles in teenage magazines that signal a return to a fifties style of game-playing between men and women, as well as numerous magazine articles delighting in stories about women declining executive positions in favour of part-time work. "Post-feminism was a catch-phrase for a while, again indicating a disillusionment with feminism," Chislett says, describing all these symptoms as "a flurry of fallout."

For the particular incident dramatized in the radio play, Chislett decided to present the story from only one perspective, that of the youngest in the quartet. "I like to have someone in radio who has a fairly clear point of view," says Chislett, adding that Kathy was to some extent drawn from a young friend of hers, who similarly practised public speaking while wandering around the house, talking aloud in a search for spontaneity. Chislett thought that this habit would make an interesting entry to a character in a radio drama, and would fit with her wish to stick with one character.

"I wanted to do something totally counter to radio's ability to travel all over time and space," she says. "I wanted to stay with the girl's mind. It's not like stage because we're where she is, we're hearing only what she hears—it has a subjectivity you can't achieve in theatre. And then I wanted to go back to a thirties theory of a slice of life, or back to Aristotle, and to set the play in real time. I wanted to take that kind of challenge, to see whether you could have a beginning, middle and an end in twenty-five minutes."

Chislett says she likes the challenges radio poses to a writer. "I enjoy writing for an individual listener," she says. "It rapidly changes the idea of humour; getting the joke in the theatre is a shared experience. You very rarely laugh aloud when you're by yourself—that's why they have laugh tracks. So in writing radio I go for the smile of recognition. It can be, at that point, a little less direct than it needs to be on the stage, although radio is not a subtle medium. It's intimate, but not subtle."

Chislett aims her work at what she decribes as "the general public," which fit neatly with the opportunity to write for the broadly-based Morningside audience. "If you come on too strong with that audience, it's gone," says Chislett. "That doesn't mean you can't say something; what it means is that you have to draw them in and entertain them, and then before they know it, get them on the train. Let them have a good time, and *then* we'll talk about the destination—and hopefully they won't mind. If you take them too far, they're just going to jump off.

"If you can just shake the certainty of one individual, then the work is worthwhile. You can't change the world, but you can give someone just the slightest little shake.... I think that the only way we can change things is by individuals getting their own history, so I tend to write for a general public with ordinary people as my characters.

"I am and remain, despite current trends, interested in social issues. I am an issue playwright and that's not a marketable thing to be. People say 'Why do you write about issues?' I answer, 'Do you want me to write about non-issues?' Although I love writing, it seems to me you go through an awful lot of pain, a lot of searching, a lot of very hard work to write. And if I do that, then I want to see something at the end that at least has the possibility of reaching an audience."

The afternoon's traumas in *Venus Sucked In* also reflect Chislett's ideas about how difficult it can be for ordinary people to create art in an ordinary day. How do you keep painting when the dishwasher is broken and relatives are on their way over for a dinner that is still raw? "We all have that question," says Chislett, adding that the issue is particularly pertinent for women. "A famous writer once said to me, 'Writing is what I do between the dishes and the laundry.' She loved that. We were talking about a male writer who had a huge desk and office, and his family had to accommodate him. Everything was geared to Daddy going into his room and working in his perfect set-up. We thought, how horrible, what pressure on him.

"Writing *is* like doing dishes. It is work."

ANNE CHISLETT was born in St. John's, Newfoundland in 1942, and attended Memorial University of Newfoundland and the University of British Columbia. She was cofounder, in 1975, of Ontario's Blyth Summer Festival, where her play *A Summer Burning* (adapted from the novel by Harry J. Boyle) was produced in 1977. She remained in theatre administration at Blyth and then Theatre Passe Muraille in Toronto until 1980, when the successful production of *The Tomorrow Box* at Ontario's Kawartha Summer Theatre encouraged her to make playwrighting a fulltime occupation. In 1982, Chislett received the Chalmers Canadian Play Award for *Quiet in the Land*; the following year this play won the Governor General's Award for Drama. Her other plays are *Another's Season's Promise* (written with Keith Roulston); *Half a Chance*; and *The Gift*, a play for young audiences. *Another Season's Promise* received the W.C. Good Award for literature on a topic of rural concern. Her stage plays have been produced in every province in Canada, and in the United States and Japan. She has also written for radio, television and film. Her radio dramas are *Yankee Notions* and *Off the Deep End*, an adaptation of *Half a Chance*—both written for Morningside Drama—and *Rat Calculus*, an original radio play aired on Canadian Free Theatre. She lives in Toronto and Huron County.

Characters

KATHY sixteen
LIZ Kathy's mother, fourty-five
BETTY Kathy's grandmother, sixty-seven
BEV Kathy's aunt, thirty-seven

The play takes place in real time. We follow Kathy throughout. Everyone else is "on" or "off" in keeping with their spatial relationship to her. Fortunately, the apartment is small, with the entrance directly into the living-room and the kitchen close by. The apartment is in a large, ordinary highrise in mid-town Toronto.

Production Credits

Venus Sucked In: A Post-feminist Comedy was commissioned by the Canadian Broadcasting Corporation for Morningside Drama and first broadcast on the CBC Radio network on May 13, 1991.

KATHY Kathleen Robertson
LIZ Susan Hogan
BETTY Charmione King
BEV Linda Griffiths

Produced and directed in Toronto by Heather Brown. Casting Consultant: Linda Grearson. Recording Engineer: Joanne Anka. Sound effects by John Stewart. Production Assistant: Kate Nickerson. Script Editor: Dave Carley. Executive Producer of Morningside Drama: James Roy.

Venus Sucked In:
A Post-feminist Comedy

Scene One

(Fantasy/speech.)

(MUSIC: Joan Baez, "Diamonds and Rust.")

(SOUND: Mike is raised. KATHY clears her throat. She adopts a public-speaking mode: quite natural and informal but with a touch of projection, opening up to an imaginary audience. She improvises the speech, sometimes with revisions and asides to herself.)

KATHY: *(Internal. Public address.)* "Women in the Nineteen Nineties." Some women in the nineteen nineties have deliberately decided to live in the world's crummiest apartment. Take my mother, for instance. If she had set out to find the place I would most absolutely hate to move in to, she couldn't have done better than this building. Her excuse is that it's in our old neighbourhood, and I'm still going to the same school. That's so I won't have *two* traumas to cope with. Well, if walking out of a perfectly good marriage and a perfectly great house were really going to make my mom into the greatest female artist since ... *(Shrug.)* I don't know who, uh ... whom ... ruining all our lives might be worthwhile. But as it is, the whole situation is just totally embarrassing. Like this afternoon, on the way back from the movie, Janet—she's my best friend—asked to come in so we could work on our speeches. I had to tell her that Sunday is now my mother's designated day for painting, and this apartment is so small her easel takes up our whole living-room. I can't even have anybody in my room, because the walls are too thin. You see, on Sunday ...

LIZ: *(Way off.)* Kath?

KATHY: *(Internal. Public address.)* ... nothing, but nothing, is allowed to disturb Mom's concentration.

LIZ: *(Off.)* Kath?

KATHY: *(To herself.)* Wait a minute ... how come the easel's covered up?

Scene Two

(Living room.)

LIZ: *(Coming on.)* Kathy, I asked you to get me a coat hanger.

KATHY: Sorry. I didn't hear you.

(SOUND: Closet door opens, coat hangers, plastic and wire; continues underneath.)

LIZ: What were you doing? Talking to yourself?

KATHY: Of course not.

LIZ: Your lips were moving.

KATHY: I was practising my public speaking. *(Passing hanger.)* Here.

LIZ: Oh, not plastic. A wire one. I want to straighten it out.

(SOUND: Rummaging through more coat hangers.)

KATHY: Are coat hangers a new painting technique or something?

LIZ: Don't be sarcastic.

KATHY: I wasn't.

LIZ: Then don't be silly. *(Going off.)* Come in the kitchen for a minute, will you?

Scene Three

(Small kitchen.)

KATHY: Mom, I kinda need to work on my speech.

LIZ: *(Coming on as KATHY nears her.)* Well, I kinda need you to hold the flashlight. *(Her voice becomes muffled as she sticks her head inside a dishwasher.)* Shine it in there where the hose connects.

KATHY: What are you looking for?

(SOUND: A coat hanger being poked into dishwasher's orifices. LIZ's voice shows the strain of arm and neck stretching.)

LIZ: Whatever's clogging this thing.

KATHY: Yech.

LIZ: Yech is right. The dishes are dirtier than when I put them in.

KATHY: Is this going to take long?

(SOUND: Clinks and clanks; continues intermittently.)

LIZ: I hope not. *(Sounds of effort as she digs at clog.)* So ... are you going to win the contest again this year?

KATHY: Not with the topic I got stuck with.

LIZ: What is it?

KATHY: "Women in the Nineties." I can't think of a single angle that hasn't been used a million times.

LIZ: You could talk about the sexism girls your age run into.

KATHY: I don't run into any.

LIZ: Sure you do. You must.

(SOUND: Clinks stop. Dishwasher door closes.)

KATHY: Not as far as I know.

LIZ: Give the dial a spin.

(SOUND: Dial turns. Mechanical sputter.)

Darn.

(SOUND: Dishwasher door opens. Clinks and clanks; continues underneath.)

What about career choices? What if you want to be an engineer?

KATHY: I don't.

LIZ: But if you did ... I can tell you I'd worry. *(Idea.)* Hey, how about gun control? There's a feminist issue for you.

KATHY: The topic is "women," not "feminism." I want it to be upbeat.

LIZ: Well ... we're sure to have a woman prime minister in a couple of years.

KATHY: I'd have a better chance with something that lets me smile a lot.

LIZ: Why? *(Outrage on the rise.)* Are the boys expected to smile?

KATHY: *(Declining the challenge.)* Look, thanks for trying to help, okay?

LIZ: No! It's not okay. Do boys look for topics that let them smile?

KATHY: How should I know! Mom, I have to be ready for the assembly tomorrow.

LIZ: Oh, Kathy. Why do you always leave assignments till the night before?

KATHY: I've been practising since Friday.

LIZ: Where? At the movies or at the skating rink?

KATHY: You were the one who suggested I call Janet.

(SOUND: Dishwasher door closes underneath.)

LIZ: Because your father disappointed you. I'd have saved my sympathy if I'd known you had a speech to write.

KATHY: I don't "write" it, Mom. I prepare it, like ... in my mind.

LIZ: In your mind?

KATHY: Yeah. It has to sound spontaneous, so I practice by making up stuff about whatever occurs to me.

(SOUND: Dial turns. Mechanical sputter.)

So, it doesn't really matter if I'm at a movie or at my desk.

(SOUND: Dishwasher door opens.)

LIZ: Good. Then it won't matter if you're at the sink, washing dishes by hand.

(SOUND: Dishes taken from dishwasher to sink; continues underneath.)

KATHY: What do we need dishes for? Aren't we sending out for pizza?

LIZ: There's been a change of plans.

KATHY: How come?

LIZ: Your Aunt Bev phoned while you were out. She invited herself to dinner.

KATHY: Oh, great!

LIZ: For you, maybe. I'd just mixed my paints.

KATHY: You could have said no.

LIZ: Well, she said she has some news ...

KATHY: Why didn't she tell you on the phone?

LIZ: She wanted to see me in person. *(Beat.)* All right, so I'm a sucker. I couldn't bring myself to say no.

KATHY: You still don't have to cook. Aunt Bev likes pizza.

LIZ: But it is Sunday. And I thought it wouldn't be much trouble to thaw a few chicken breasts.

(SOUND: Water taps turned on, water running; continues underneath.)

That was before I discovered there wasn't a clean pot or pan in the kitchen.

KATHY: *(Hesitant.)* Mom? ...

LIZ: What?

KATHY: Maybe ... if you called Dad, he'd come over and fix the dishwasher?

LIZ: *(Dismissive.)* Come on, Kath, pick up a tea towel.

KATHY: He's probably finished at his office by now ...

LIZ: Oh, don't be silly.

KATHY: I bet he could have that thing working in five minutes flat.

(SOUND: Taps turned off.)

LIZ: Kathy, you want to know about women in the nineties? I'll tell you about women in the nineties. They've ended up alone at forty-five in rotten cheap apartments, with rotten lazy superintendents. They've been brought up to believe they are utterly hopeless when confronted with a mechanical problem. But women in the nineties are going to learn to make it on their own! They will wash every dish in the city of Toronto before they will ever again trade their personal integrity for some jerk who knows how to repair appliances.

KATHY: Cute, Mom.

(SOUND: Aggressive dishwashing; continues underneath.)

Except I think the principal would dock me for false generalization.

LIZ: The principal is a man, naturally.

KATHY: No, she's a woman. It's just no big deal with her.

LIZ: What's no big deal?

KATHY: She doesn't think men are all jerks. And she's not paranoid about them trying to keep her in chains, either.

LIZ: I'm paranoid? Is that what you're saying?

KATHY: Well ... I mean ... maybe some men did try to keep your generation down.

LIZ: Maybe?

KATHY: Yeah, but the principal's younger, so her attitude is more "now."

LIZ: What do you mean "now"?

KATHY: You know, more like Aunt Bev's than like yours.

LIZ: *(Flaring.)* Really! Then you should ask your Aunt Bev for help, shouldn't you?

(SOUND: Dishwashing fades out.)

Scene Four

(Fantasy/speech.)
KATHY: *(Internal.)* Sisters. *(Public address.)* "Women and their Sisters." *(An afterthought.)* "In the Nineties." Have you ever seen that Bell Canada commercial? The one where this girl calls her sister because she needs a soft shoulder? Well, those two girls are definitely not my Mom and Aunt Bev. I figure it's because Mom is jealous. You see, Aunt Bev has her "personal integrity," which in my mother's mind means her chosen career, whereas Mom wasted fifteen years doing graphic art just to make money. She says that was Dad's fault because he insisted on a middle-class lifestyle. Except now, without him, she has to waste even *more* time on commercial stuff to pay the rent. The thing is Aunt Bev makes twice as much money at her journalism, *and* she's got a great guy too. Sam not only does his share of the housework, he makes all their meals, on top of bringing her a long-stem rose every day. In other words, he's exactly the kind of guy Mom wanted my dad to be. But the weird thing is: Mom is always down on Aunt Bev for putting her own desires before anyone else's ... which is exactly what Mom walked out on Dad so she could do herself. Not that she does. In fact, my mom can find more reasons not to do what she says she wants than anybody I ever heard of. *(To herself. Idea.)* Hey ... maybe ... I could make a really fun speech about her totally screwed-up behaviour. Yeah ... like ... my mother says her art is going to be a priority in her life ... that is unless ... let's see ...

Scene Five

(Kitchen.)
(SOUND: Dishwashing fades back up; continues underneath.)
KATHY: So, Mom, how much painting did you get done today?
LIZ: I told you. I hadn't touched the canvas when the phone rang ...
KATHY: *(Internal. Public address. Following her train of thought.)* Unless the phone rings.
(SOUND: Apartment intercom buzzer; off.)
LIZ: What are you mouthing?
KATHY: That's the buzzer.
LIZ: Not already. Get it, will you?

(SOUND: Dishwashing noises recede.)

Scene Six

(Entrance way/living-room.)
(SOUND: Apartment intercom buzzer.)
KATHY: *(Presses "Talk.")* Who is it?
BETTY: *(Through intercom.)* The Queen of England.
KATHY: Mom, what's Granny doing here?
(SOUND: Apartment intercom buzzer.)
LIZ: *(Coming on.)* For heaven's sake, press the door button.
KATHY: *(To intercom.)* You have to wait for the middle elevator. *(To LIZ.)* Did she phone and invite herself too?
LIZ: I phoned her.
KATHY: I see.
LIZ: I thought if I was cooking for you and Bev ... I might as well cook for Mother.
KATHY: Mom, do you realize we've been here two months and you haven't finished one single picture?
LIZ: I would have today ... if the dishwasher hadn't screwed up.
KATHY: I guess dishwashers want to keep women in chains too.
LIZ: That's a very snide remark.
KATHY: Well, you always blame Dad for not letting you paint. It seems to me *(Quoting.)* "the problem is simply your own lack of commitment."
LIZ: Is that what your father told you?
KATHY: I mean, look at this afternoon ...
LIZ: Yes, look at it! Who is supposed to take you out of my hair on Sunday?
KATHY: It's not Dad's fault he had to work.
LIZ: Kathy, I will not tolerate any quotations from that jerk about my lack of commitment, understand!
KATHY: What makes you think Dad said it?
LIZ: You didn't come up with an idea like that by yourself. If it wasn't your father, who was it?

KATHY: If you must know, it was Aunt Bev.
(SOUND: Knock on apartment door; off.)
LIZ: *(Taken aback.)* Bev told you I lacked commitment?
KATHY: I heard her tell Gran ...
LIZ: Now come on. You're making that up.
(SOUND: Knock on apartment door.)
KATHY: Here's Gran. Since you don't believe me—
LIZ: *(Overlapping.)* Kathy!
KATHY: ... you can ask her yourself.
LIZ: *(Overlapping.)* Kathy!
(SOUND: Door opens.)
KATHY: Hi, Gran. Mom wants to—
LIZ: *(Overlapping.)* Don't you dare!
BETTY: *(Off.)* Elizabeth, what's wrong?
LIZ: Nothing, Mother. Come in.
(SOUND: Door closes underneath.)
BETTY: *(Moving on.)* I could hear you two shouting since I left the elevator.
LIZ: We were having a discussion. The door is paper thin.
BETTY: Yes, I suppose. *(To KATHY.)* Kathy, I'm surprised to see you home on a weekend.
KATHY: Dad had a computer crash.
BETTY: *(Judgemental.)* I see.
KATHY: *(Defensive.)* Well, he couldn't help it.
LIZ: Come and sit down, Mother. I'll move my easel ...
(SOUND: Easel moved underneath.)
BETTY: Oh, are you trying to paint again?
LIZ: What do you mean "trying"?
BETTY: *(Beat.)* Trying to find time, of course. May I see it?
LIZ: *(Defensive.)* No! *(Recovering.)* Not yet. Not until it's finished. Open the closet door, Kath.
BETTY: Beverly and Sam aren't here yet?

(SOUND: Closet door opens. Rattle of coat hangers as easel is put in; continues underneath.)

LIZ: Actually ... Sam had to go see his father. He's back in hospital.

BETTY: I was wondering why Beverly was honouring us with her presence.

LIZ: *(Laughing.)* You couldn't expect her to cook her own dinner. Speaking of which ... I'd better get to it.

BETTY: May I give you a hand?

LIZ: No, no ... you and Kathy have a chat.

KATHY: Mom, I need to work on my speech.

LIZ: Perhaps your grandmother can help you.

KATHY: It's about women in the *nineties*, remember?

LIZ: Kathy!

BETTY: Never mind. *(Moving off.)* I'm going to inspect your balcony for a bit.

LIZ: Mother, you haven't been here three seconds.

BETTY: *(Off.)* Yes, but I couldn't smoke in the cab either.

(SOUND: Standard apartment balcony door opens. Hum of city noise, very low. Door closes.)

LIZ: For Pete's sake, Kath, your speech has waited this long. Go out and try to be nice *(Moving off.)* for a change.

KATHY: In a minute, okay?

Scene Seven

(Fantasy/speech.)

KATHY: *(Internal.)* Anyway, where was I? Oh, yeah. *(Public address.)* "Women's Confusing Behaviour." Teachers always tell us to talk about what we know, and the woman I know best is my mother. Well, I find the way she acts very confusing. She says her art is important, but not as important as answering the phone, fixing the dishwasher, or making dinner. Like today with Aunt Bev ... Mom could have told her she was busy. I mean, I understood since I was a kid, if Dad has to work, he has to work, and there's no sense whining about it. I have to admit I didn't mind Mom being there. But it's like Dad says ... if you want something you have to go get it. I guess the point is ... well ... if women want to—no. If women *in the nineties* want to get ahead in the world, I mean if they want to make it as artists or something, then they better not act like my mom. They should act like my dad instead. *(To herself.)* Not bad ... but it's kinda ... it's a downer.

Scene Eight

(Living room.)

LIZ: *(Off.)* Kathy!

KATHY: I'm on my way.

(SOUND: Balcony door opens. Hum of city noise; continues underneath.)

Scene Nine

(Balcony. Flick of cigarette lighter.)

KATHY: Gran, are you on your *second* cigarette already?

BETTY: *(Puffs.)* If it bothers you, feel free to go inside.

KATHY: *(Ironic.)* Great view, eh? If you like parking lots.

BETTY: Perhaps your mother will find a nicer neighbourhood. *(Puffs.)* When your house is finally sold.

KATHY: Dad says if Mom forces him to sell in today's market, we won't even cover the mortgage.

BETTY: Kathy *(Beat.)* shouldn't you be working on your speech?

KATHY: Well ... *(Becoming intimate.)* I'm sort of making one up about Mom, but ...

(SOUND: Balcony door closes. City noise continues underneath.)

Gran, do you believe Mom has a chance of becoming famous?

BETTY: Well, she was "quite well known" once. She even had a one-woman show.

KATHY: Oh, that. *(Meaning ancient history.)* That was before I was born.

BETTY: Really? What a coincidence.

KATHY: *(Takes point.)* Okay, Gran. But women with commitment manage to have kids *and* a career. That is, if they have talent too.

BETTY: I think your mother has talent.

KATHY: *(Very intimate.)* Go take a peek at that canvas in the closet ... just take a peek.

BETTY: I wouldn't dream of doing such a thing without permission!

KATHY: Gran, it's gross, really gross. The whole canvas is this nude woman ... being swallowed by an oyster!

BETTY: *Rising* from the oyster, surely. Like *Venus Rising*?

KATHY: No ... she's being swallowed ... the body is all stretched out and her mouth is open like she's screaming. Believe me, nobody, but nobody, in his right mind is ever going to buy it.

BETTY: I'm not an expert in modern art, and I doubt if you are either.

KATHY: Gran, please ... listen, for Mom's own good, don't you think you should have a talk with her ... you know ... about the divorce?

BETTY: Kathy, I'm hardly in a position to give anyone advice.

KATHY: But you're her mother!

BETTY: I know I am. That's why she has to invite me over on Sunday afternoons. Now, if you've nothing more to say, I'm going back inside.

(SOUND: Balcony door opens. City noise continues for a moment, then fades.)

Scene Ten

(Fantasy/speech.)

KATHY: *(Internal. Public address.)* "Grandmothers in the Nineties." Grandmothers in the nineties aren't what they're supposed to be. They aren't grey-haired, they aren't loving, and they're no help to their granddaughters at all. *(To herself.)* Boy, is that ever a dead end.

(SOUND: Apartment buzzer; off. Hum of city noise comes up underneath.)

Maybe Aunt Bev ... if I can get her alone ... *(Calling to LIZ.)* It's okay, Mom. I'll answer it.

(SOUND: City noise fades.)

Scene Eleven

(Entrance way/living-room.)

KATHY: *(To intercom.)* What's the password?

BEV: *(Intercom.)* Chocolate Orange Ice Cream.

(*SOUND: Door buzzer.*)

KATHY: *(To intercom.)* Alright! *(To LIZ.)* Mom, I know you were joking when you suggested it, but would you be mad if I do a speech about Aunt Bev?

BETTY: I suppose you can't get more nineties than your aunt.

LIZ: *(Comes to kitchen doorway.)* The "me" generation belonged to the seventies, Mother.

KATHY: She's "now" enough to buy gourmet ice cream, and she does have a perfect relationship.

LIZ: *(Moves back into kitchen.)* Oh sure ... without any "commitment" on either side.

KATHY: *(Calling.)* I knew you'd be mad.

LIZ: *(Off.)* I'm not mad. I'm putting the potatoes on.

(*SOUND: Angry rattle of pots; off.*)

BETTY: Kathy, you aren't thinking of telling your class about Beverly and Sam, are you?

KATHY: Why not? Oh, Gran ... lots of people don't bother with marriage anymore. At least if she and Sam break up they don't have to go through a divorce.

BETTY: No, and your aunt will get even less out of the ordeal than your poor mother.

KATHY: Relationships are about love, Gran. Not money.

BETTY: Life is never so simple as when you're sweet sixteen.

KATHY: You don't have to patronize me.

BETTY: Then *you* stop patronizing *me*.

LIZ: *(Coming on.)* What's going on? Kathy, are you being rude?

KATHY: She always talks to me as if I were a child.

BETTY: And she talks to me as if she knows the answers to everything. Well, you don't, little girl. You don't even know the right questions.

LIZ: Oh, come on, you two!

KATHY: Mom, what does she mean?

(*SOUND: A knock.*)

LIZ: Nothing, Kathy. Nothing that concerns *you!*

(*SOUND: Door opens.*)

(Tense.) Hi, Bev. Come in.

BEV: *(Panting.)* Liz, what's wrong?

(SOUND: Door closes.)

(Panting.) I could hear you three shouting from halfway down the hall.

LIZ: We were having a discussion.

BETTY: It seems the door is especially thin.

BEV: *(Starts to breathe more normally.)* The door may be, but the tension in here is ten feet thick.

BETTY: Beverly, dear, you sound like you ran up the stairs.

BEV: Yes, I missed my workout this morning.

(SOUND: Closet opens, rattle of hangers; continues underneath.)

LIZ: *(Slightly off.)* Bev, I've put your stuff in the closet, okay?

(SOUND: Closet door closes.)

BEV: Oh wait, there's a bottle in my bag ...

(SOUND: Closet door opens.)

(Slightly off.) Hey ... is that your painting stashed in there?

(SOUND: Closet door slams.)

LIZ: Yes, it's stashed! Whose fault do you think that is?!

BEV: What?

LIZ: I had no "lack of commitment" till you phoned!

KATHY: Mom!

BETTY: Girls, are you arguing already?

LIZ: Mother, stay out of this!

(SOUND: Clinking pot lid and hiss of water boiling over in kitchen; off; continues underneath.)

BEV: *(Confused.)* Stay out of what?

LIZ: *(Moving off.)* Damn. The potatoes!

BETTY: Let me—

LIZ: *(Off.)* No, no, I'll take care of it.

BEV: Liz, I'm getting the feeling I'm not welcome here.

(SOUND: Clanks, hiss; off.)

LIZ: *(Coming back on.)* Bev, I've had a bad day ... I shouldn't have said anything.

BETTY: *(Changing subject.)* Beverly, your gourmet ice cream must be starting to melt.

BEV: Oh, well, I'll put it in the freezer. *(Beat.)* Here ... *(Hands LIZ bottle.)* I brought us wine.

BETTY: Good. Your sister could use a drink.

KATHY: *(Sotto.)* Mom, can I have a few minutes, just Aunt Bev and me?

LIZ: Okay, Kath, I'll stay out of the kitchen.

Scene Twelve

(Kitchen.)

BEV: *(Coming on.)* So kiddo, not out with Daddy today?

(SOUND: Freezer door closes.)

KATHY: The system at his office went down.

(SOUND: Cupboard door opens and closes.)

BEV: *(Knowing.)* Uh huh.

KATHY: It's not fair of Mom, you know. She only gives him one chance a week.

BEV: *(Calling.)* Liz, all I see in your cupboard is mugs.

LIZ: *(Off.)* Oh lord, the wine glasses are still in the dishwasher.

(SOUND: Dishwasher door opens.)

(Coming on.) Hand me a few. I'll give them a rinse.

BEV: What's wrong with the dishwasher?

LIZ: It's broken.

(SOUND: Taps, running water.)

KATHY: Aunt Bev, how would you define a nineties woman?

BEV: Oh, I'm not into definitions. *(Referring to dishwasher.)* Liz, want me to take a look inside?

(SOUND: BEV fiddles with the insides of the dishwasher, speaking with her head inside it.)

LIZ: *(Annoyed.)* There's no point fooling with it.

BEV: I bet all this needs is a straightened-out coat hanger.

LIZ: I have one right here.

(SOUND: Clinks and clanks; continues underneath.)

BEV: Perfect.

LIZ: *(Over the last, insistent.)* I tried that, Bev.

BEV: *(Head still in there.)* Liz, trust me.

KATHY: *(Trying to get in.)* So ... Aunt Bev ...

BEV: So, Kath ... *(Yielding with a sigh.)* What kind of woman do you have in mind? Black women, Native women ... Third World women ...

KATHY: I guess ... women like *you*.

LIZ: Middle-class white liberal yuppies.

KATHY: White liberal?

BEV: That's a sixties phrase, kiddo.

(SOUND: One big final clink.)

(Coming out of dishwasher.) I think I've solved the problem.

LIZ: It means people who think they can solve problems they know nothing about.

(SOUND: Dishwasher door closes.)

BEV: Turn it on.

(SOUND: Dial is turned. Dishwasher behaves perfectly.)

(Triumphant.) There!

LIZ: *(Amazed.)* What did you do?

(SOUND: Dishwasher turned off. Dishwasher door opens.)

BEV: I'll show you.

KATHY: *(Internal. Public address; over BEV and LIZ.)* The true nineties woman, not like my mother, but exactly like my Aunt Bev, is not hopeless when confronted with a mechanical problem.

BEV: *(Underneath KATHY's speech.)* This hose was completely clogged.

LIZ: I figured that ... but I couldn't get at it.

BEV: It takes a bit of flexibility.

KATHY: *(Internal. Public address.)* She exercises regularly so she looks *twenty*-eight years younger ... well, at least eighteen younger than Mom, instead of only eight. And ...

BEV: Our kitchen had a machine like this before we remodelled.

LIZ: I sure envy you that kitchen.

BEV: Sam loves cooking in it.

KATHY: *(Internal. Public address.)* Oh, yeah. Early in life she refused to learn to cook or to type, so she cannot be forced into any stereotypical roles such as Mother used to complain about.

BETTY: *(Coming on.)* Why is everyone in the kitchen?

BEV: Liz and I are talking, Mother.

(SOUND: A pot clinks.)

LIZ: Mother, what are you doing?

BETTY: Turning up the element.

LIZ: *(Irritated.)* I just turned it down.

BETTY: But the potatoes have stopped boiling.

LIZ: *(Angry.)* For God's sake, I know how to cook potatoes.

BEV: Mother, why don't you go and sit down? We'll bring your wine in a minute.

BETTY: *(Moving off.)* As you wish.

KATHY: *(Internal. Public address.)* The nineties woman can take charge of any situation without sounding crabby like Mom.

(SOUND: Rattle of cutlery drawer.)

BEV: Liz, where's your corkscrew?

LIZ: Oh, no ...

KATHY: *(Internal. Public address.)* And also, unlike my mother, Aunt Bev would never forget to buy important things like corkscrews ...

LIZ: Kathy, the Seven Eleven will have one ...

KATHY: *(Cool.)* I'm busy at the moment, Mom.

LIZ: *(Moving off.)* Oh, for the love of heaven.

KATHY: *(Internal. Public address.)* The nineties woman is the perfect person to make the sixties woman see that it's too late for her to change her life now.

BETTY: *(Slightly off.)* Liz, where are you going?

LIZ: Out!

(SOUND: Apartment door opens.)

BETTY: *(Slightly off.)* Wait for me.

(SOUND: Apartment door closes.)

(In hall, off.) Liz, you may think you're coping, but it looks to me as if ...

BEV: Lord, the door really is thin.

KATHY: Anyway, Aunt Bev, now that we have some peace ...
BEV: Kath, to tell you the truth, women's issues don't turn me on.
KATHY: Don't worry ... I've got that done ... I want you to give me your honest opinion of something entirely different.
BEV: What?
KATHY: In the living-room.

Scene Thirteen

(Living-room.)
(SOUND: Closet door opens, cloth is taken off painting.)
KATHY: Here in the closet.
BEV: *(Coming on.)* What are you doing?
KATHY: Look, Aunt Bev ... look what Mom has been working on for almost two months.
BEV: *(Astonished.)* My lord ...
KATHY: So ... what do you think?
BEV: *(She hates it.)* Well, I don't know much about painting.
KATHY: Do you like it?
BEV: *(Beat.)* Is that the title on the bottom? *(Giggle.)* The bottom edge I mean?
KATHY: Where?
BEV: "Venus Sucked In" ... oh, I see. Now it makes sense.
KATHY: It does?
BEV: Yes, I think there's a famous painting on this subject.
KATHY: Gran mentioned it ... *Venus Rising*?
BEV: I only remember a Joan Baez song about Madonnas on the half shell ...
KATHY: That was before my time.
BEV: It was before my time too but your mother was a great fan of Joan Baez. I guess this painting is some kind of parody.
KATHY: You mean it's a joke?
BEV: Your mother may be working out her hostility. The shell must represent old-fashioned male expectations of women.

KATHY: Yeah, but in terms of now ... do you think Mom can make it as an artist or not?

BEV: The subject matter is self-indulgent ... and ... perhaps a bit dated in its aggressive feminist metaphor.

KATHY: You mean it's crap.

BEV: Well ... it might work for today's market if her approach were less literal and a bit more ... playful.

KATHY: It's crap, Aunt Bev.

BEV: Oh. *(Beat.)* Anyway, I think we should put it away before she gets back, don't you?

(SOUND: Painting is put back. Closet door closes.)

KATHY: What I think is that you should come straight out and tell Mom that she should throw out her oil paints and go home where she belongs.

BEV: It's a bit late for that, kiddo.

KATHY: No! The divorce isn't final. Legally they're still married.

BEV: But they don't want to be.

KATHY: Only because Mom's being selfish. I mean, Aunt Bev, maybe it's great for you being single, but you don't have a kid.

BEV: Actually, I might soon.

KATHY: Really? You want to have a baby?

BEV: I'm going to have one.

(SOUND: Door opens.)

KATHY: You mean *you're* pregnant?

LIZ: *(Coming on.)* You're pregnant?

(SOUND: Door closes.)

BEV: *(Sotto.)* Oh, lord, where's Mother?

LIZ: Gone, to the store by herself, she wanted more cigs anyway.

BEV: Thank god ... with her, I need to announce my wedding plans first.

KATHY: You're getting married?

LIZ: *(Mournfully.)* I thought the last thing you ever wanted was to be tied down.

BEV: *(A light tone.)* I'm not going to be tied down.

KATHY: *(Overlapping.)* She doesn't have to be tied down.

BEV: I can afford a nanny, and Sam's promised to do his share of the parenting.

LIZ: Bev, you've no idea of what you're getting into.

BEV: Oh, Liz, I knew you'd be like this about it.

LIZ: Like what?

BEV: Negative, bitter. Look, it's Sam's idea, and he'll make a wonderful father. He's not like your Dave, you know.

KATHY: What's that supposed to mean?

BEV: Oh, nothing, kiddo.

LIZ: Kath, how about you go see what's keeping Gran?

KATHY: *(Overlapping LIZ.)* Dad *is* a good father ... he's a good father.

LIZ: Of course he is. Now, Kathy, I want to talk to your aunt alone.

KATHY: I'm not leaving if you're going to say mean things about Dad.

LIZ: Please, Kathy, do as you're told.

KATHY: Okay.

Scene Fourteen

(Hallway.)

(SOUND: Door opens and closes.)

BEV: *(From other side of door.)* Funny how kids are devoted to people who don't give a shit about them, isn't it?

LIZ: *(Under KATHY's speech.)* Hush ... she might hear you.

KATHY: *(Internal.)* Tell her she doesn't know what she's talking about. Dad loves me. You know he does.

LIZ: I find it heartbreaking, and there's nothing I can do about it except try to protect her.

BEV: She's going to see through those computer breakdowns sooner or later.

KATHY: *(Internal.)* What's that supposed to mean?

BEV: What if she runs into him out with one of his bimbos sometime? I told you I ran into him last Sunday, didn't I?

KATHY: *(Internal.)* No! No! It's not true.

LIZ: Yeah, you told me.

KATHY: *(Internal.)* Maybe ... it was somebody from work ... maybe he was so lonely ...

LIZ: *(Overlapping KATHY.)* She'd probably find a way to excuse him. She'll probably say I drove him to it.

BEV: Why do you put up with it? If a kid of mine criticized me the way she criticizes you, I certainly wouldn't stand for it.

LIZ: She's been hurt enough already.

KATHY: *(Internal.)* I'm not going to cry.

LIZ: Or maybe I'm a coward. Maybe I'm scared she'll say I deserved to be dumped ...

KATHY: *(Aloud.)* Dad walked out on her ... *(Internal.)* He dumped *her*?

LIZ: Maybe I'm scared she'll make up a speech about how her mother is such a fool ... such a loser ... such a statistic!

KATHY: *(Internal.)* Oh, Mom ...

BEV: *(Overlapping KATHY.)* Liz, for pity's sake. You have to stop getting sucked into what other people want from you. You have to learn to make yourself your own priority.

LIZ: My daughter has always been my priority. I'm too old to change now. You can't have a child and still put yourself first, Bev. And if you intend to try, maybe you should commit yourself to running up a lot of stairs in the next few months.

BETTY: *(Coming on.)* Kathy ... what are you doing?

KATHY: Gran ...

LIZ: *(Calling from other side of door.)* Who's out there? Kathy?

KATHY: *(Sotto.)* Gran, pretend we met by the elevator, okay?

BETTY: Why? What's the matter?

KATHY: *(Over her.)* Please, Gran ... trust me ...

(SOUND: Door opens.)

LIZ: Kathy, you weren't eavesdropping, were you?

KATHY: No! I was waiting by the elevator.... Gran was on it when it came.

BETTY: *(Beat as she decides whether or not to go along.)* Here you are. One corkscrew.

(SOUND: Door closes.)

Scene Fifteen

(Living-room.)

BEV: Give it to me, I'll pour.

LIZ: Kath, would you like half and half with soda?

KATHY: No, thanks, Mom.

LIZ: But we have to drink a toast to your Aunt Bev.

(SOUND: Cork extracted, glasses, wine pouring.)

BEV: *(Upbeat.)* Mother, you'll be thrilled to know I've finally said yes to Sam.

BETTY: That's wonderful!

LIZ: Kath, where are you going?

KATHY: To my room.

BETTY: Aren't you going to even congratulate your aunt?

KATHY: Congratulations.

LIZ: Sweetheart, you look upset.

KATHY: I'm fine, Mom. I just have to do that speech.

BEV: I thought you said you had it done?

KATHY: I changed my mind.

LIZ: *(Slightly off.)* Okay, Kath. I'll call you when dinner's ready.

KATHY: Yeah, thanks.

BETTY: *(Fading off.)* Beverly, tell us your plans. You're not being married in white, are you?

Scene Sixteen

(Internal and from kitchen.)

KATHY: *(Internal.)* Who needs to write a book about Aunt Bev anyway.... Maybe Mom's idea was better ... yeah.... *(Public address.)* In the nineteen nineties, we are sure to have a woman prime minister.... What that will mean for women everywhere ... or for our planet ... or for girls growing up ... I don't really know. You take my Aunt Bev. To be honest I don't think she'd be any better than the men.

BEV: *(Slightly off.)* Liz, I'm starved. Did you ever put the chicken in the oven?

LIZ: *(Slightly off.)* Oh, look, you guys wouldn't like pizza, would you?

BETTY: If it's less trouble.

BEV: *(Slightly off.)* I could have stayed home and had pizza.

KATHY: *(Internal. Public address.)* Because she only thinks about herself.

LIZ: Okay, okay ...

KATHY: *(Internal. Public address.)* Of course, someone like Mom might be different. So what if she can't get around to her painting, or even if she's any good at it.... She really cares about other people ... and that's what would be most important. I mean, what I'm saying is ... that whether a woman prime minister is going to make a difference or not, well, it depends on the woman, that's all.

(MUSIC: Joan Baez up and out.)

Mussomeli–Düsseldorf

by Dacia Maraini

translated by
Margaret Hollingsworth

Tradition and rebellion seem to be themes as central to DACIA MARAINI's life as they are to her writing. She comes from a family of writers—her Irish grandmother wrote travel books and traversed the globe, her anthropologist father authored a number of books—and she speaks of this as "a line in the family, a tradition. I knew when I was a child that I wanted to write." But early on, her writing caused a stir in the publishing world. When she was twenty-five, her second novel, published in English as *The Age of Malaise*, won the important Formentor Prize (1962), but was deemed too risqué to be published in Spain, one of the six awarding countries.

That novel features a disaffected teenage girl caught in a "modern malaise." It was hailed as a daring exploration of the sexual meanderings of the generation that was to flower in the sixties. Margaret Hollingsworth, who translated *Mussomeli–Düsseldorf*, says that this figure of a precocious, almost obnoxious young woman who challenges every system comes up again and again in Maraini's dramas. Certainly the daughter in *Mussomeli–Düsseldorf* is on the attack against her mother and the double standards of her parents' generation. Placing female characters from traditional and modern cultures side by side on a train journey between

Italy and Germany gave Maraini another chance to explore areas where societies overlap and seperate.

"Many of my stories are sort of a sentimental education, sentimental-sexual," says Maraini. "I'm quoting the book by Flaubert, *Sentimental Education*, about the life of a young girl who grows up in a society in which she's very uncomfortable about all the different values and things that happen to her. This is one of the things in my books. I write about men and women, naturally, and women and women, but not in an ideological way. I don't believe so much in ideology."

Another of the conflicts between cultures in the play comes from the issues raised by large-scale emigration, a theme which crops up in much of Maraini's writing. "Italy is full of different types of people and different languages and different habits which meet and sometimes don't meet, and confront, sometimes violently," she says. Italy's long history of emigration, particularly from Sicily to more prosperous parts of the world, has meant many adjustments in the society, both for the men who leave for work and the women who stay home. While emigration to such countries as Germany has slowed in recent years, the newer trend of immigration to Italy raises similarly complex questions about how cultures clash or coexist.

"I think that modern life in a big town is more and more about conflicts between different cultures," says Maraini. "In Italy, we have Africans, people from the Philippines, from Turkey, who come to do work Italians don't want to do any more. But you can't treat them like machines—they are people and they bring with them their culture." Maraini says she thought this particular play would speak clearly to the Canadian experience as well.

"More and more in the big industrial towns, the multicultural situation is becoming important," says Maraini. "There is always a problem of living together. This happens in families too, because many times in a family you can find people with different experiences and different ideas of how to live." In *Mussomeli–Düsseldorf*, these differences include the mother's idea of faithfulness to one man, an absurd concept according to the daughter, who sees only that her father has another life and that her mother's version of her marriage is false. Although not heard from in the drama, the father is a character caught in the middle, trying to bridge the two worlds. "He belongs physically to the new culture where he is working, but he's linked to the ancient, traditional culture—and he can't decide," says Maraini. "That's the problem. The daughter would like him to decide, or the mother to decide, but it is very difficult to deal with these two mentalities."

"The mother pursues the idea of the traditional family, the ideal family, which doesn't exist. The daughter wants her to understand that this kind of family is only in her imagination," Maraini says, adding that things are changing in Italy, but slowly. "The mother is changing, all the mothers are changing, though we still have such a difference in Sicily," says Maraini, who has lived on the island off southern Italy. (Her mother comes from Sicily, her father from Tuscany.) "In Sicily, you can find some things which belong to the very distant past, archaic family situations, and at the same time you find modern, emancipated women."

Maraini says her sympathies aren't automatically with the daughter in this play. "The two women belong to different cultures. The traditional, regional culture and the modern, advanced, emancipated culture—I'm not saying that one is better than the other. Both have something that is worth keeping. But sometimes they can't exist together. It's very difficult.

"I have sympathy for the mother, also for the daughter. She is for clearness, for being honest and not pretending. The mother thinks the father is always there because he belongs to the family, because he is the chief of the family. The daughter wants her to understand that the father is already participating in another culture, another world."

The train is one connection between the two cultures, the large, industrialized city (Düsseldorf) and the small country village (Mussomeli). The third character, the train's ticket collector, interrupts the argument between the two women as they cross such a large distance, culturally and geographically. "The ticket taker is the person who breaks this very strong tension between the two women. He breaks the atmosphere," says Maraini. "He is like the train—the train stops and the stop is a break in the journey. He represents the normality of a person who doesn't really make decisions. He just lives."

Maraini wrote this play specifically for radio, and says that she doesn't often transfer stories between radio and stage. "The suggestiveness of sound on radio is very important, is primary. When I write for the radio I always think in terms of sound," she says, adding that the train is a crucial element that wouldn't translate to another medium. "This play wouldn't work in the theatre, because the theatre is much less suggestive in the sense of sounds. The train is sound and rhythm, and in the theatre even using a false wagon wouldn't give you the idea of moving."

In *Mussomeli–Düsseldorf*, the journey between the two countries, like the confrontation between the two cultures, does not end. "I leave it open," says Maraini. "I write to understand, not to tell what is right and what is wrong—because I don't know. I try to understand, so my writing is a sort of journey in the dark."

DACIA MARAINI was born in 1936 in Florence, Italy. She is one of Italy's pre-eminent playwrights and cultural figures, author of more than twenty-five stage plays and many radio dramas, as well as a number of novels and books of poetry. Daughter of the noted Orientalist scholar, Fosco Maraini, she lived in Japan for eight years, until age nine. In her mid-twenties, she received early encouragement for her writing from Alberto Moravia. Her second novel, *L'Eta del Malessere (The Age of Malaise)*, won the prestigious Prix Formentor in 1962 and has been translated into twelve languages. Other awards include Premio Saint Vincent (1972), Premio Riccione (1978) and Premio Arta Terme (1983). She has published several volumes of poetry. In 1970 she directed a film adaptation of the Alberto Moravia novel, *Conjugal Love*. Her most widely translated and produced stage plays include *Two Women of the Province, Dialogue Between a Prostitute and One of Her Clients, Mary Stuart, Norma 44, Tableau of the Troupe, Stravaganza, The Dreams of Clytemnestra* and *Giovanni Tenorio*. These plays, which explore themes of sexuality, violence, power and the family, have been translated into several languages and produced throughout Europe and Latin America, and in the United States and Australia. Since 1967 she has also founded and run a number of theatre companies, most recently Compagnia della Magdalena, which operated for eighteen years. Established in 1973 to produce plays by women, the company continued until 1990 as a centre for seminars on feminist issues, particularly those related to playwrighting. She lives in Rome, and travels a great deal.

MARGARET HOLLINGSWORTH was born in Sheffield, England in 1939 and emigrated to Canada in 1968. Her stage plays include *Mother Country* (1980), *Ever Loving* (1981) and *War Babies* (1985). Two collections of her short plays have been published, *Wilful Acts* (1985) and *Endangered Species* (1988). Her stage plays have been produced in Canada and England, and her radio plays have aired on the CBC and the BBC, as well as in West Germany, Australia and New Zealand. A volume of her short stories, *Smiling Under Water*, was published in 1989.

Characters

DAUGHTER seventeen
MOTHER fifty-five
TICKET COLLECTOR fifty

The play takes place in a compartment in a moving train. The Italian card game *scopa* uses a deck with a suit called cups.

Production Credits

Mussomeli–Düsseldorf was commissioned by the Canadian Broadcasting Corporation for Morningside Drama and first broadcast on the CBC Radio network on May 22, 1991.

MOTHER Clara Hare
DAUGHTER Josephine Stebbings
TICKET COLLECTOR Wendell Smith

Produced and directed in Edmonton by Kathleen Flaherty. Recording Engineer: Eric Wagers. Sound effects by Dean Purvess. Production Assistant: Ivan Todosijczuk. Script Editor: Dave Carley. Executive Producer of Morningside Drama: James Roy.

Mussomeli–Düsseldorf

(SOUND: Train, fades underneath.)

DAUGHTER: Go on, throw out the ace of clubs and I'll pick up the jack of cups. Let's see what that gives us—

MOTHER: It gives us—scopa.

DAUGHTER: But all the queens are out!

MOTHER: No way—I still have one in my hand.

DAUGHTER: You always beat me.

MOTHER: I'm hungry. D'you feel like a sandwich?

DAUGHTER: Not right now. C'mon, let's have another hand.

MOTHER: We've been playing all day. Let me have a little rest. D'you want a cookie?

DAUGHTER: No.

MOTHER: Some wine?

DAUGHTER: This journey's gonna go on forever—it feels like we've been on the train for a week.

MOTHER: It's only twelve hours. How about some orange juice?

DAUGHTER: Come on, one more little game—

MOTHER: Oh all right, shuffle the cards—

DAUGHTER: It's done ... here, three for me, three for you ... do you think Papa'll be glad to see us?

MOTHER: We'll be a surprise.

DAUGHTER: Papa hates surprises.

MOTHER: He'll love this one.

DAUGHTER: What if he's not alone?

MOTHER: When the wife arrives all the other women leave.

DAUGHTER: Mamma, you just threw out the settebello! And I'm grabbing it. That's one point to me.

MOTHER: Nice work, Mariuccia.

DAUGHTER: What if he asks you for a divorce?

MOTHER: He'd never do that—he loves you too much.

DAUGHTER: Me?

MOTHER: A child can't grow up without a father.

DAUGHTER: I'm seventeen, Mamma, I'm not a child—anyway, where is this great father of mine? I've only seen him about twenty times in seventeen years!

MOTHER: He's made so many sacrifices just to be with you—always on the road—Mussomeli Düsseldorf, Düsseldorf Mussomeli—in the beginning he spent six months here and six months there.

DAUGHTER: And every time he came home he brought you a mountain of washing—shirts, socks, and underwear, and towels—

MOTHER: And I did it happily—it told me he was all alone up there.

DAUGHTER: And that he couldn't be bothered to go to the laundry.

MOTHER: He didn't want anyone else touching his things.

DAUGHTER: I'm never gonna get married, Mamma.

MOTHER: I said the same thing when I was your age.

DAUGHTER: I mean it.

MOTHER: You'll change your mind.

DAUGHTER: You're lucky, you know that? You never have to look anything in the face.

MOTHER: So, how do I look, huh?

DAUGHTER: *(Affectionately.)* Like a fool!

MOTHER: Oh, that comes naturally after you've been around as long as I have.

DAUGHTER: But you're not a fool. You've taken your medicine like a good girl, and you'll go on taking it—but I'm not gonna do that, Mamma, I hate medicine.

MOTHER: Oh, you will ... then after that maybe you'll kiss a frog.

DAUGHTER: I remember how beautiful you used to be—with your almond-shaped eyes—and when you wore your hair down over your shoulders. Now look at you, your hair's dry and dull, and you wear it all bundled up as if you're afraid it'll escape on you. And your eyes are dead—the almonds are dried up.

MOTHER: My body's aging, getting ugly—what do you expect with three grown sons, one baby dead by the time he was three, and another at four, two miscarriages—sometimes I've felt like a station, everyone coming and going.

DAUGHTER: If I ever got married I'd find myself a rich salami maker.

MOTHER: Ach, you'll change your tune when you fall in love.

DAUGHTER: Didn't I fall in love with Rito? We made love, and when he asked me to marry him I told him to get lost.

MOTHER: Ach, it'd've been another story if you'd got pregnant....

DAUGHTER: If I'd got pregnant I'd've had an abortion.

MOTHER: You mustn't talk like that. You know it's a sin.

DAUGHTER: Mamma, sometimes you sound like you came out of the ark.

MOTHER: Oh come on, play, throw out that seven of clubs you're holding—

DAUGHTER: How did you know I have the seven?

MOTHER: Oh, we have good memories in the ark.

DAUGHTER: What if Papa really does ask you for a divorce this time?

MOTHER: He swore before Saint Anthony.

DAUGHTER: Do you think Saint Anthony gives a damn about Papa?

MOTHER: He's never let me down.

DAUGHTER: Saint Anthony?

MOTHER: No, your father—he's honoured his vows.

DAUGHTER: But can't you see that it's turning him into a schizophrenic? One woman in Mussomeli, another in Düsseldorf, one daughter in Sicily and one in Germany.

MOTHER: A bastard in Germany.

DAUGHTER: And you want him to have to say he fathered a bastard, poor guy. Is that how you punish him?

MOTHER: There. You've let me make a point with this little two of cups. That's the last hand. I'm the winner.

DAUGHTER: I know. You always beat me. Talking, playing—you name it—

MOTHER: Oh you've seen me playing while I talk. Me and the neighbours sitting around playing cards and talking about our husbands.

DAUGHTER: If he gives you a divorce you'll be free—you could find another husband.

MOTHER: You only get one husband—one husband and one soul.

DAUGHTER: Your sister Teresa was married twice.

MOTHER: She'll pay for it in the next life.

DAUGHTER: What next life? Isn't one life enough for you? You want another?

MOTHER: We'll always be called upon to make reparations—

DAUGHTER: Okay, do you have any more cards up your sleeve? You've won the last four games, I'm just left with the settebello.

MOTHER: You see, a little retribution for your sins.

DAUGHTER: I don't think God gave me the wild card. I dealt it to myself.

MOTHER: Everything comes from God.

DAUGHTER: Okay, so no divorce. Poor old Papa, you've really cut him down to size ... a poor old man who wakes up in the night sweating and pleading: "Am I here, or am I there? Who am I married to? Giuseppina or Inge?"

MOTHER: Every man I know has a wolf lurking inside him—it pops out every so often, lusting for flesh. They're worse in Sicily. I'd never want to turn my Tano into one of those horrible Sicilian wolves. I like him tethered the way he is. But he has to respect his legitimate wife.

DAUGHTER: Let's have another hand, Mamma.

MOTHER: You haven't let me look out of the window for a single moment. I don't even know where we are.

DAUGHTER: What's it matter? We're still on the way to Düsseldorf.

MOTHER: Look—a river! Look how wide it is! Back home all our rivers are wrinkled up little trickles.

DAUGHTER: It must be the River Po.

MOTHER: I've never seen such a wide river—bursting at the seams—it's incredible.

DAUGHTER: It's filthy.

MOTHER: Oh you! Look at the bank there—those trees, jumping with life, and those little white waves ... so white—they look like they've been washed in bleach.

DAUGHTER: You said it, they've been washed in detergent. Tons of acid, and poisons—there isn't a single fish left in that water, there isn't even a frog—not a tadpole, nothing.

MOTHER: Oh, don't be such a wet blanket.

DAUGHTER: Come on—play.

MOTHER: Is it really the Po?

DAUGHTER: Ach, the Po or the Adige, it's all the same thing.

MOTHER: I like the train because it cuts right through the countryside, and we can stretch out inside. Planes make the fields look stupid, and vineyards all look like children's toys from up there.

DAUGHTER: But planes get you there faster.

MOTHER: There's a sin of pride in flying—it compresses time, and makes you look down on things.

DAUGHTER: I guess you're right. You have brains, Mamma, what I'd like to know is how come you never made it as a teacher. You know, I remember when you used to be rushing out—early in the morning with your arms full of books—you were so beautiful—concentrating so hard—you were fresh as a new day.

MOTHER: Oh Lord, I was expecting Antonio. Don't you remember my belly? Then Stefano put in an appearance, then Tonino.

DAUGHTER: It's stupid to have so many kids! You're so old-fashioned, the pair of you. You're clinging to all the old ways—like the peasants in Mussomeli—all the old grannies.

MOTHER: It was what kept us together. Without kids I'd've been a permanent grass widow. But this way—each year there was this knot that tied us together in spite of the distance.

DAUGHTER: This is just your obsession with proving to the world that you're his legal wife—nobody cares any more ... nobody cares.

MOTHER: I care, and that's enough. I care, and God cares.

DAUGHTER: You and God—what a pair! What's poor old Papa meant to do? Just carry on, grit his teeth, and hide, like a wolf in his lair—and what about poor old Inge? He wants to marry her.

MOTHER: She's a free woman. What's marriage to her?

DAUGHTER: There are laws, papers—things your God doesn't even know about.

MOTHER: I've stood my ground for twenty-five years, do you want me to lose everything now?

DAUGHTER: You could shake off the chains, find a boyfriend.

MOTHER: Who do you think's gonna get turned on to me? A fifty-five-year-old woman.

DAUGHTER: You don't have to wait for someone to get the hots for you. You have to make the first move.

MOTHER: It's not decent, Mariuccia. A woman of my age. I'm not meant to be thinking about love any more.

DAUGHTER: But why? Are you meant to be a corpse?

MOTHER: Only God knows how I look with no clothes on. Your father hasn't seen me naked for more than ten years.

DAUGHTER: But you still make love ...

MOTHER: Fully clothed. Or under the covers ... in the dark.

DAUGHTER: You're nuts! Nuts!

MOTHER: Oh—it still feels very nice.

DAUGHTER: No one can be in love with one man for so many years. You've changed—both of you. He's with another woman. He speaks another language. He smells different. Haven't you noticed he doesn't even walk the same way any more?

MOTHER: I like him just the way he is. As far as I'm concerned he hasn't changed at all.

DAUGHTER: You're crazy!

MOTHER: Oh, get away. You sound like an old lady and you're only just seventeen.

DAUGHTER: Seventeen today isn't like seventeen in your day.

(SOUND: TICKET COLLECTOR opens the door and enters.)

TICKET COLLECTOR: Tickets please.

DAUGHTER: Oh, you can't want to see them again. The other guy was just through here.

TICKET COLLECTOR: Passengers are required to show their tickets whenever they are requested to do so.

DAUGHTER: You sound like a textbook.

MOTHER: But he's right—how does he know what the other man saw? Are you married, sir?

TICKET COLLECTOR: *(Taken aback.)* Of course I'm married.

MOTHER: Yes, you look like you're married. Do you have children?

TICKET COLLECTOR: *(Uncertain whether to take this as a joke or be shocked.)* Two, a boy and a girl.

DAUGHTER: Two—at least that's normal, not eight like you!

TICKET COLLECTOR: *(Attracted by MOTHER and deciding that levity is called for.)* You have eight children, Signora?

MOTHER: Beh, I've only got one right now. Her. I have three in Canada staying with one of their uncles. He's financing their studies. Two died when they were babies, and we lost two more before they were born.

TICKET COLLECTOR: Well, all this child-bearing has done nothing to diminish your looks.

MOTHER: What looks? I'm just an old cast-off.

TICKET COLLECTOR: Nonsense. You're a beautiful woman. Just look at those twinkly eyes.... May I buy you a coffee?

MOTHER: No thank you ... I never accept coffee from strangers.

DAUGHTER: But he's not a stranger. He's the ticket collector. Anyhow it was you that spoke to him first. Go on Mamma, I'll stay here and read.

MOTHER: I can't possibly. It's too hot—

TICKET COLLECTOR: There's air-conditioning in the bar.

DAUGHTER: Really?

TICKET COLLECTOR: I don't have much to do today. The train's almost empty. I just have to get to the end of this carriage and then turn around. So—shall we go?

MOTHER: No thank you. Would you like to have a hand of scopa with me?

TICKET COLLECTOR: I don't know how to play scopa. I'm not from the south.

MOTHER: Then join us in some wine from my vineyard. We make a dark red wine with a bouquet like crushed flowers.

TICKET COLLECTOR: Why not? I'll go check the end of the train and then come back—that way I can rest easy. Thanks.

MOTHER: I've got a beautiful piece of ham from our pig. Poor old Gino was such a friendly guy—he used to wake me up in the mornings with his grunting—he always followed me when I went into the vineyard. I hated having to kill him.

TICKET COLLECTOR: I'll be right back.

(SOUND: Door opens and closes. Murmurs from people passing in corridor.)

DAUGHTER: Hey, you've made a conquest ... he's not a bad-looking guy either, even with no hair and yellow teeth. Why don't you give him a bit of encouragement?

MOTHER: Don't be silly.

DAUGHTER: He likes you.

MOTHER: Isn't that odd? I wasn't expecting it after I told him about my eight kids—an old lady like me—everyone's always so respectful in

Mussomeli. No one'd ever dare to proposition Tano Calo's wife—the man who emigrated to Germany.

DAUGHTER: You're still a good-looking woman, Mamma, and you've buried yourself alive for a man who's started a new family with a new woman.

MOTHER: Don't talk about your father like that—God gave me one husband, and I'll keep him until the end.

DAUGHTER: That's how priests talk.

MOTHER: Being a wife is a bit like being a priest. You keep your faith with the church and the family; you make sure you stay chaste and you keep busy with your children or your lost sheep.

DAUGHTER: Wives! There's nothing to being a wife!

MOTHER: Nothing to it? Is that why I've put in twenty-five years learning how?

DAUGHTER: And by the time you've figured it out you're left on your own.

MOTHER: I always set a place for him at the table. Every time I change the sheets, I put out clean pillowcases for him. Every time I have a glass of wine, I put out a glass for him.

DAUGHTER: *(Gently.)* If we can't change the world, it's because of people like you, Mamma—you all stick like barnacles to your old prejudices.

(SOUND: Door opens and closes as TICKET COLLECTOR returns.)

TICKET COLLECTOR: May I?

MOTHER: Please. Sit yourself down. Have you come for a glass of our wine?

(SOUND: Wine being poured into glass.)

TICKET COLLECTOR: Take a look at that colour! Rubies, liquid rubies. *(Drinks.)* It's like dried figs, new-mown grass, excellent! I haven't drunk anything like it since ...

MOTHER: Drink up. Have some more. I'm just taking a few bottles to my husband.

DAUGHTER: Let's have a toast to the latest pregnancy of Father's German wife.

TICKET COLLECTOR: *(Ironically.)* Your daughter's got a good sense of humour. *(Beat.)* What's your name?

MOTHER: Her name's Mariuccia.

TICKET COLLECTOR: No—*your* name, Signora.

MOTHER: Mine? Giuseppina ... isn't it awful? They're all called Giuseppina or Antonina back home—where do you come from?

TICKET COLLECTOR: *(Proudly.)* I'm from Rocca Pagana.

MOTHER: Where's that?

TICKET COLLECTOR: Near Avellino. Do you know that part of the world?

MOTHER: No.

TICKET COLLECTOR: They're all called Giuseppina or Antonina where I come from as well. I gave the name to my daughter. But we call her Pina. What do they call you?

MOTHER: Oh, my family calls me Pinuccia. *(Laughs.)*

TICKET COLLECTOR: *(Closing in.)* You should let your hair down, it'd give you new life. I'll bet it's really long.

MOTHER: My daughter says it's dry and lack-luster.

TICKET COLLECTOR: You're joking! Your hair's beautiful. And there's so much of it. How can anyone have so much hair? Look at me—I'm almost bald—I started losing my hair when I was thirty—pretty soon I'm gonna look like a billiard-ball.

DAUGHTER: Sampson lost his strength when he lost his hair.

TICKET COLLECTOR: Not me—I can honestly say I've got stronger since I started losing my hair. I never catch colds, and I toss the mail bags as if they were twigs—and when I take a woman in my arms ...

MOTHER: Do you often take women in your arms?

TICKET COLLECTOR: No. Not my wife. My wife spends all her time sleeping.

MOTHER: What do you mean, *all* her time?

TICKET COLLECTOR: She's no sooner awake in the morning than she's asleep again—at lunchtime she eats, and then she falls asleep. She cleans the house, irons, washes and falls asleep—she sleeps in front of the TV.

DAUGHTER: Maybe she's waiting for the prince to kiss her and wake her up.

TICKET COLLECTOR: Yes, you'd have to say something like ...! Oh, excuse me, Signora.

DAUGHTER: Keep your hair on. You old people are all the same. You can't take a joke. My father's that way too—

TICKET COLLECTOR: *(Turning back to MOTHER.)* What does your husband do?

MOTHER: Oh, he was just a labourer for years. Then he got to be foreman. Now he's in management—he gets paid very well.

DAUGHTER: He has to, to keep up two houses, one in Mussomeli and one in Düsseldorf. Not to mention two wives, one who's with us— Giuseppina, and one who isn't—Ingeborg Shaffer di Regensburg.

MOTHER: Men are like that. They spread themselves out.

TICKET COLLECTOR: We men don't like to be tied down—we're slaves of the flesh.

DAUGHTER: Slaves of the flesh? What bullshit!

TICKET COLLECTOR: You obviously don't think very highly of me, Signorina.

DAUGHTER: Me? A moment ago I was telling my mother that you're a good-looking guy in spite of being bald. Right Mamma?

MOTHER: Right. She was encouraging me to—to ... *(Laughs.)*

TICKET COLLECTOR: To flirt with me a little?

DAUGHTER: No. To screw you.

MOTHER: Don't use those words, Mariuccia, do you want to shock the man?

DAUGHTER: Anyone want another glass of wine? Don't take me seriously, I like to joke around.

TICKET COLLECTOR: To be honest, I'd never take advantage of you, Signora—

MOTHER: You know, you've just made me want to get to know your wife. She must be a very nice woman.

DAUGHTER: Even if she is a sleepwalker.

TICKET COLLECTOR: Don't let's talk about my wife—it depresses me.

MOTHER: So who shall we talk about?

TICKET COLLECTOR: Let's talk about you.

MOTHER: Me?

TICKET COLLECTOR: Do you mind if I tell you that you have the most beautiful eyes I've ever seen in my life?

MOTHER: My daughter tells me they're like two dried almonds.

TICKET COLLECTOR: They're two jewels, so shiny, so alive.

MOTHER: Oh, they're only two old mother's eyes.

TICKET COLLECTOR: And you actually made this wine?

MOTHER: You should see us when we're in the vats, with our skirts round our waists and our feet all stained with the red juice ... there's me, and Marta, the lawyer's daughter, and Morena, my son Stefano's mother-in-law, we sing and crush the grapes—we have so much fun.

TICKET COLLECTOR: It must be wonderful.

DAUGHTER: She comes back to the house at night drunk and giggly, with her ankles all swollen and cut, stinking of fermented grapes—d'you know that smell, it's the worst!

TICKET COLLECTOR: *(Amorously.)* And do you keep hens?

MOTHER: Oh, a dozen or so—they all have their own names. There's Granny and Hunchback and Pizza Margherita—they're all a bit on the small side ... and then there's himself—Dudu the cock. He's got a red comb, to see him is to love him.

TICKET COLLECTOR: Does he make good eggs?

MOTHER: A bit smaller than the ones you'd buy in the store, but the taste ... they have a nutty flavour, as sweet as you please—right, Mariuccia?

DAUGHTER: They smell of shit.

MOTHER: *(Laughing.)* Sure, sometimes they do. We dry them off—we eat them all, shit or no shit. I don't know if my hens are particularly brainless, but they sure are greedy. If you let them range free they eat everything in sight. One day the eggs'll smell of fish, another of beans, another of onions—one day we gave them orange peels, and guess what, the eggs came out smelling of oranges.

TICKET COLLECTOR: I'm gonna come and nose you out. I'm always on the move in this train in any case, up and down, south to north, north to south—it's called the Settebello. Sicily to Milan.

MOTHER: The Settebello. So you liked my wine eh?

TICKET COLLECTOR: I'm gonna come and gorge myself.

MOTHER: Oh, don't bother. I'll mail you a few bottles, or put them on the train. *(Laughs.)*

TICKET COLLECTOR: Oh, but I won't only be coming for the wine. I'll be coming to find you.

MOTHER: You'd come looking for me in Mussomeli, way up in the Sicilian mountains?

TICKET COLLECTOR: Where else?

MOTHER: *(Remembering who she is.)* You seem to have forgotten that

I'm a married woman, and I cannot permit a man to come looking for me while my husband's away.

DAUGHTER: There we go, he's no sooner got started than you have to ruin it all.

MOTHER: You know very well that I could never ...

TICKET COLLECTOR: Calm down, no one needs to see me.

MOTHER: Fat chance—even the walls have ears where we live.

TICKET COLLECTOR: Then why don't you come to me?

MOTHER: I won't even discuss it.

TICKET COLLECTOR: What if we meet some place halfway, some place where no one knows us?

MOTHER: He's proposing that we have some kind of illicit affair—like your father.

DAUGHTER: Well, why not? He's doing it. You should go for it!

MOTHER: *(With decision.)* Let's drink another glass of this good red wine sir, then you can go back to work. I have a husband, and I'm in love with him.

TICKET COLLECTOR: I don't understand faithful women, but I admire them. My wife is faithful. She's a complete mystery to me. I'm not going to insist dear lady ... but I'll give you my address. If you change your mind, write to me—I'll see what can be done.

MOTHER: Thank you—you've been very kind—you've made me feel young again—I'm very grateful to you.

TICKET COLLECTOR: You have the most beautiful hair in the world, and such sparkling eyes—goodbye, Signora. Goodbye, Signorina.

DAUGHTER: Goodbye.

(SOUND: Door closes as TICKET COLLECTOR leaves. Train clatters along.)

DAUGHTER: You're an idiot, Mamma. That guy woulda married you.

MOTHER: But he has a wife.

DAUGHTER: She sleeps all the time. I think he'd divorce her in a second if you asked him to.

MOTHER: I told you. One life, one husband. Subject closed.

DAUGHTER: But if you liked him—you did, I could see from the way you laughed—your eyes really did start to sparkle and your hair came tumbling down all on its own. It broke out of that knot you tied it up in, and all its old colour and shine came back—

MOTHER: Oh, don't talk nonsense, Mariuccia—I'm an old lady.

DAUGHTER: Eating him up. He was bug-eyed over you, didn't you see that?—he was head over heels and you sent him away—it was a walkover, Mamma!

MOTHER: I intend to sleep with your father tomorrow.

DAUGHTER: But he doesn't intend to sleep with you. Don't you understand?

MOTHER: Of course he does. We make love every time we get together.

DAUGHTER: He does it out of duty.

MOTHER: Oh, you people can't tell the difference between duty and pleasure.

DAUGHTER: The pleasure of being in charge of your own life again?

MOTHER: He loves me in his own way.

DAUGHTER: What a way.

MOTHER: What do you know? Maybe you've been living with him for twenty-five years like me, huh?

DAUGHTER: You haven't lived with him for twenty-five years. If you strung all the days he's been with you together, you wouldn't even come up with two years. He's been in Düsseldorf all the time, and he's always had other women.

MOTHER: But I'm his wife.

DAUGHTER: He's scared of you, Mamma, he knows how you think. He's put you and God in the same boat. You make a terrible pair.

MOTHER: Let's not forget the Madonna. She talks to me sometimes at night.

DAUGHTER: The Madonna's just another dream.

MOTHER: She tells me to hang on, stay pure for her sake, and for him—

DAUGHTER: Well, at least you're tempted—your body isn't completely dead.

MOTHER: Michele wanted me—Michele the farmer—he ran after me for a whole year—he waited for me behind the chicken coop, he followed me into the vineyard, and he always had presents, shawls, bracelets, once he even had a bottle of French perfume.

DAUGHTER: So it's not true that the guys back home don't dare come onto you.

MOTHER: I'd've said no even if he was expiring with love. If I'd accepted him your father would've been scarred for life. Anyway I sometimes thought Michele was doing it to discredit your father, then maybe buy the land at half price—

DAUGHTER: You're always putting yourself down. Why couldn't he have been madly in love with you?

MOTHER: Even if he had been, he had no right to tell me. He knew I wasn't free. It was an insult to your father.

DAUGHTER: What's the use? You're as stubborn as a mule. It's hopeless! You're lost to humanity.

MOTHER: You make me laugh, Mariuccia—you're just like your father—it all has to be so dramatic.

DAUGHTER: It's you who's always play-acting. If I like someone I tell him. It's easy. All these stories about word of honour and untouchable matrimonial vows make me want to throw up!

MOTHER: Ach, you've made me dizzy with all this chatter.

DAUGHTER: It's the wine that's made you dizzy, not me.

MOTHER: No way—I hope I'm used to my own wine. I drink it every day and it's never made me dizzy.

DAUGHTER: Okay, so you got drunk on that guy's sweet nothings.

MOTHER: Look—the moon's out—it's struggling, poor thing—it's hardly shining at all—it seems to be held up there by a single thread.

DAUGHTER: I've never heard you talk about the moon. Love works wonders!

MOTHER: Oh, I never have time to look up when I'm at home.

DAUGHTER: Come on—let's have a little game.

MOTHER: Let me look out the window for a while—I love this time of evening.

DAUGHTER: What is there to see? Come on, let's play.

MOTHER: You won't be put off, will you? Go on, shuffle the cards—whose turn is it?

DAUGHTER: Mine. Here we go ... three cards for you ... three for me.

(SOUND: Voices fade. Fade up sound of train.)

The Making of Warriors

by Sharon Pollock

SHARON POLLOCK uses a striking image to illustrate her concerns about how to tell a story from a perspective that is not her own. "It's as if truthfulness when you're writing about life is a big multi-faceted diamond. I am standing in one place, and I am the result of a certain time and place and experience, and I have a flashlight. If I never try to expand those boundaries I can only hold my flashlight one way, shine it on one part of the diamond. By being aware of how I do see through certain eyes and in a certain way, I get to expand, I get to be able to move the light.

"But I can't go all the way around that diamond. So when I tell the story of Walsh or Sitting Bull, I may be shining my flashlight on a certain portion of that diamond. The First Nation person who is beside me is in a different place, but the same position I am. I suppose when you have many writers attacking the same story, you get the entire diamond lit up.

"I think that I can write a story so long as I find a way within the structure of the story to acknowledge my angle of observation. I'm the result of my middle-class, white upbringing in a conservative part of the country, in a racist country, in a colonized country, next to the largest, most powerful country in the world. I am aware of that and I try to educate myself and sensitize myself to how that has formed me, so that

I can understand and overcome the limitations that it's put on me—but to believe that I could ever manage to get rid of all that is a great lie."

Pollock was asked to write for Morningside Drama at a time when she was growing increasingly troubled about the struggles of First Nation peoples in Canada. She had been personally involved "in a small way" with the Teigan people and the fight against the Old Man River damn in Alberta. That and violence at Oka, Quebec and elsewhere in the summer of 1990 started her reading widely about Native issues and history. One of the books she read was about a Micmac woman from Nova Scotia, who was murdered in South Dakota in 1976 shortly after the Wounded Knee episodes. Despite her great interest in Anna Mae Pictou Aquash, Pollock said she could at first see no truthful way to write about a Native woman's life and death.

Then she began to think of Morningside's programming style, its mingling of subjective and objective perspectives; every day the program's combination of interviews, panels, reports and single-voice stories covers a wide range of political, social and cultural issues. Pollock thought a similar structure would provide a way into the story. "I thought I could have voices that are speaking directly to the listener, some of it seeming like objective news, some of it seeming like very subjective experience and some of it dramatization," she says. "Maybe I *could* tell Anna Mae's story without assuming the voice of the other, by making it objective and making evident my white perspective as much as possible."

While continuing to look for stories where she felt she could "assume more closely the voice of the other without pretending to be 'the same as'," Pollock remembered reading about Sarah Moore Grimke, a nineteenth century American activist who was among the first to draw a link between black slavery and the oppression of women. Connections between the two lives kept emerging as Pollock read about this "lost figure" and other suffragette history. "Certain phrases from my reading jumped out at me," says Pollock, "economic and religious and societal philosophies and theories that were supposed to justify the position of women, the institution of slavery, and in fact that we use today to justify the ongoing injustice that First Nation people suffer."

The Making of Warriors handles these stories, these issues, by balancing subjective and objective voices. One extreme is the very personal voice of the woman Pollock acknowledges as representing herself in the drama, the fifty-four-year-old white woman who has an almost magical experience driving through the Pine Ridge Reserve. "It's an experience I actually never had, but *believe* I have because I've created it for myself," says Pollock. On the other end of the spectrum is the more objective voice that presents the facts of Anna Mae Pictou Aquash's life, though even it becomes more engaged as the details accumulate. Pollock says she decided not to use a Native voice for that narration because she didn't want any implication that she was telling the story from that viewpoint.

Pollock describes *The Making of Warriors* as three stories: "Here are three women saying, we're going to tell you a story, or we're going to tell you three stories. One says, 'I'm going to tell you a very personal story about what happened to myself one day in February.' Another voice is saying, 'I'm going to tell you a story about a woman who lived in the past, and once upon a time,' and then there's the dramatization. And the third voice, which I think of much more as the newspaper reporter, says, 'This happened! This happened! This happened!' And so there are three stories told three different ways that intersect—and the three voices have a reason for telling the stories. And the reason for telling the stories is 'Come on, let's do something, let's get going.'" The play ends with a very strong "urge to action," which Pollock sees as fitting into the context of the series and the Women Playwrights Conference.

In writing a drama based on these two lives, Pollock also dealt with her continuing concern about how to portray women characters truthfully, without endorsing the status quo or pretending that everything works out just fine. "In the world we live in injustice prevails. It's very difficult for women to triumph," says Pollock. "So how do you write a story about a woman emerging triumphant without trivializing or diminishing the real nature of the struggle, which is so great, the anguish, the struggle from which so many of us fail to emerge victorious? And once you get to win, what do you do then? Then it becomes glorification, propaganda."

One way around this, Pollock felt, was to have the narrators participate in the drama and invite their audience to do the same. This continues the stories, making it clear that what Sarah Moore Grimke and Anna Mae Pictou Aquash worked for didn't die with them. "It seemed to me that I was able to find in Sarah somebody who I could talk about continuing on triumphant for a bit, and at the same time make it clear that Anna Mae had triumphed too," says Pollock. "I'm juxtaposing the literal facts of their deaths with the metaphysical or symbolic meaning of their living on. And the women on the Pine Ridge Reserve change; they move forward into some kind of collective action. That's when the voices come together."

Pollock plans to expand this work into a stage play, with a second act that may introduce different contemporary characters who have somehow taken up the challenge of that call to action. She is interested in what happens when women join to fight for change, how principles are challenged when put into practice by a diverse group with many different agendas. "The women's movement doesn't often admit inequities and differences among its various constituencies," says Pollock. "Basically, there are so many women with a larger voice or a louder voice or a bigger piece of the pie who don't want to examine how the pie gets divided up. If you just want a bigger piece, you're not going to examine whether perhaps the pie shouldn't be cut the same way at all."

SHARON POLLOCK was born in Fredericton, New Brunswick in 1936, and grew up in Quebec's Eastern Townships. She began writing for the theatre in 1967. She has been the recipient of several major awards, including two Governor General Awards for Drama: for *Blood Relations* (1981) and for *Doc* (1986). These and her other plays, including *Compulsory Option*, *Walsh*, *And Out Goes You?*, *The Komagata Maru Incident*, *One Tiger to a Hill*, *Getting It Straight* and *Whiskey Six Cadenza*, have been produced by every major theatre in Canada. Her many radio dramas include adaptations of *Walsh*, *The Komagata Maru Incident* and *Doc*, and such original radio plays as *Sweet Land of Liberty*, awarded a Nellie for Best Radio Drama in 1981. She has written several plays for children and television scripts, including *The Person's Case*, winner of the 1981 Golden Sheaf Award. In 1988, she won the Canada-Australia Literary Prize. She has been Artistic Director of Theatre Calgary and Theatre New Brunswick, and Associate Director with both the Stratford Festival and the Manitoba Theatre Centre. She lives in Calgary.

Characters

WOMAN ONE	informal, conversational tone, fifty-four
WOMAN TWO	formal, neutral, factual tone, thirties
WOMAN THREE	warm, "storytelling" tone, thirties
SARAH	ages ten to eighty, (b.1792–d.1873)
FATHER	Sarah's father, fifty-five
MRS. BRENT	Sunday School supervisor, forty
THOMAS	Sarah's brother, ages fifteen to thirty
ANGELINA	Sarah's sister, ages ten to seventy
MALE VOICE	authoritative
WELD	Angelina's husband, mid-thirties on first appearance

A dash at the end of a line indicates an interruption, rather than a pause; overlapping words are enclosed in square brackets. WOMAN TWO is in narrative space, except when in the car.

Production Credits

The Making of Warriors was commissioned by the Canadian Broadcasting Corporation for Morningside Drama and first broadcast on the CBC Radio network on May 20, 1991.

WOMAN ONE	Tanya Jacobs
WOMAN TWO	Kate Trotter
WOMAN THREE	Ann Farquar
SARAH	Jill Frappier
THOMAS	Bruce Clayton
MRS. BRENT	Nonnie Griffin
ANGELINA	Maureen McCrae
MALE VOICE	Frank Perry
WELD	Tom Butler

Produced and directed in Toronto by James Roy, Executive Producer of Morningside Drama. Chanting and drumming by Jani Lauzon. Casting Consultant: Linda Grearson. Recording Engineer: Glen McLaughlin. Sound effects by Matt Willcott. Production Assistant: Nina Callaghan. Script Editor: Dave Carley. (Note: The scene with Sarah's father was not included in the CBC production because of time constraints.)

The Making of Warriors

Scene One

(MUSIC: Native drums.)
WOMAN ONE: The making
WOMAN TWO: of warriors
WOMAN THREE: the making
WOMAN ONE: of warriors
WOMAN TWO: the making
WOMAN THREE: of warriors
WOMAN TWO: an exploration of
WOMAN THREE: a story about
WOMAN ONE: a personal reminiscence
(MUSIC: Drums end.)

Scene Two

(Inside car.)
(SOUND: Car door opens.)
WOMAN THREE: Come on.
WOMAN TWO: Now.
WOMAN ONE: Now.

(SOUND: Car door closes; key in ignition; engine turns over; car pulls away. We are inside.)

Now listen. I ... *(Small chuckle.)* I ... am a white woman. Age? Age fifty-four. A little overweight. I don't mind saying that. Well, I do, but I am. So. *(Another chuckle.)* So.

WOMAN TWO: Anna Mae Pictou Aquash is a Native woman. A Micmac. On March 27th, 1976, Anna Mae will be thirty-one years old. She usually calls home at Christmas, and on her birthday.

WOMAN THREE: In 1792 Sarah Moore Grimke was born in Charleston,

South Carolina. Sarah's father was Chief Justice of the Supreme Court of that state.

WOMAN ONE: On February 24th, 1976, thirty days before Anna Mae's thirty-first birthday, I drove through the Pine Ridge Reserve in South Dakota on my way to Route 90. Near Wanblee I passed a group of men. White men. About ten or twelve of them standing by the side of the road. They were just ... standing there. I remember because they stared at me, at the car, as I passed. I slowed down. I didn't stop. Why should I stop? I was just ... passing through. On my way. Somewhere. To Route 90. I think.

WOMAN THREE: The Grimkes were an upper ... class family. They owned a large plantation. They owned a lot of slaves. Black people.

WOMAN TWO: The Micmac Reserve near Shubenacadie, Nova Scotia, where Anna Mae Pictou Aquash is born on March 27, 1945, does not provide a solid economic base for the people who live there. Native people. Micmac people. Aboriginal people.

WOMAN ONE: Red.

WOMAN TWO: People.

WOMAN ONE: I saw something red. I didn't stop. But the moment stuck.

WOMAN THREE: Sarah Grimke didn't fit in South Carolina.

(SOUND/MUSIC: Car cross-fades with the sound of single-note scales played on a harpsichord; continues underneath WOMAN THREE's speech.)

Sarah had "unwomanly aspirations" for a white woman whose father was a judge in South Carolina in the seventeen and eighteen hundreds.

WOMAN TWO: Anna Mae does not achieve academically in the Canadian school system.

WOMAN THREE: Even as a child, Sarah's character was termed "unnatural." Sarah Grimke—

(MUSIC: Chord on harpsichord.)

SARAH: *(In her old age.)* Slavery marred my comfort from the time I could remember myself.

Scene Three

(Outdoor afternoon social.)
(SOUND/MUSIC: Harpsichord in background, murmur of voices, clink of glasses.)
SARAH: *(At age 16. Off.)* Papa!
FATHER: It'll be a grand crop this year—
SARAH: *(Off.)* Papa!
FATHER: ... mark my words, Mr. Stanton, a grand crop.
SARAH: *(Off.)* Papa! Hurry Papa!
FATHER: Excuse me sir. *(Lowers voice.)* Thomas.
THOMAS: Yes Papa?
FATHER: Is that young Sarah callin' out?
THOMAS: Sounds like it ... and here she comes, skirts hiked up and runnin' like a— [deer]
SARAH: *(Approaching.)* Hurry, hurry up! Papa, hurry up!
FATHER: Quiet down, child, we've guests.
SARAH: You have to hurry, Papa, down back a the field kitchen, hur-ry!
FATHER: Slowly, Sarah, slowly.
SARAH: Yes Papa.
FATHER: Now what is it?
SARAH: Joeboy is back a the field kitchen and he's beatin', he is beatin' one a the girls from the house, Papa, he is beatin' and beatin' her with a, with a—
FATHER: Lower your voice, Sarah.
SARAH: ... and the blood is runnin' down her back and you've got to make him stop, I tried to and he just—
FATHER: Thomas.
THOMAS: Yes Papa?
SARAH: I've run all this way and she's not cryin', she's not sayin' a word and Joeboy says you told him to do that and—
FATHER: Take your sister inside.
SARAH: ... and you've got to stop him!
THOMAS: Come on, Sarah.
SARAH: Joeboy says she was slippin' food again and—

FATHER: Go along with your brother, Sarah.
SARAH: ... and Joeboy said you said it was the second time and—
FATHER: That's enough.
SARAH: ... he was s'posed to do that—
FATHER: Sarah!
SARAH: ... beat her like that, you said so!
FATHER: Go inside with your brother!
SARAH: But—
FATHER: And when you can behave like a lady—
SARAH: ... he said—
FATHER: ... your mother and I'd be happy to have you join us.
SARAH: But Papa!
THOMAS: Come on, Sarah.
SARAH: But—

(SOUND/MUSIC: Harpsichord and social fade out as THOMAS speaks.)

THOMAS: You sound and look a sight. Shame on you, in front a everybody like that. *(Moving off.)* What on earth were you thinkin' of, Sarah?

Scene Four

WOMAN TWO: *(Narrating.)* In 1960 Aboriginal people in Canada get the vote. In 1962 Anna Mae Pictou Aquash leaves school. That summer and fall she picks blueberries and harvests potatoes as a migrant worker. She lives in a tarpaper shack. She sleeps on a straw pallet. She moves to Boston.

Scene Five

(Sunday School room.)
(MUSIC: Chord on harpsichord.)
MRS. BRENT: Miss Sarah?
SARAH: Yes Mrs. Brent?
MRS. BRENT: I ... ah ... want to say how, how grateful we are to have a young lady like yourself givin' of her time at the Sunday School for Blacks.

SARAH: I enjoy it.

MRS. BRENT: Yes. Well. We do appreciate what you're doin' here, but ... but, a problem has arisen.

SARAH: What problem?

MRS. BRENT: You do understand that you are responsible for the oral instruction a the catechism—

SARAH: To teach the catechism, yes I—

MRS. BRENT: ... to give oral instruction in the catechism—

SARAH: ... yes to—

MRS. BRENT: ... orally instruct—

SARAH: ... to instruct—

MRS. BRENT: *(Exasperated.)* I notice you *showin'* the catechism to the children.

SARAH: Well yes.

MRS. BRENT: *Showin'* it to them.

SARAH: Yes.

MRS. BRENT: The *pages* a the catechism.

SARAH: Yes.

MRS. BRENT: *(More exasperated.)* Miss Sarah, the meanin' a the word "oral" in "oral catechism" means "oral"—

SARAH: I learnt my catechism through the readin' a the catechism, Mrs. Brent, and I thought—

MRS. BRENT: Slaves can't read, Miss Sarah.

SARAH: Well that's what I'm—

MRS. BRENT: Slaves can not read.

SARAH: I am teachin' them to— [read the catechism]

MRS. BRENT: You are to share your knowledge a the catechism orally with the children, there is no readin' here, there is no teachin' to read here, there is no learnin' to read here, there is none a that here! Slaves can't read! And I think you know that, Miss Sarah!

SARAH: I'm ... sorry, I ... I ...

 (MUSIC: Chord on harpsichord.)

Scene Six

(Parlour.)

SARAH: I am sooo aggravated.

THOMAS: Oh Sarah.

SARAH: *(Mimicking.)* Oh Thomas.... Well I am. Aggravated. Because slaves *can* read.

THOMAS: Slaves can't read.

SARAH: I've taught Kitty to read.

THOMAS: You have not.

SARAH: I have so, and it took no time at all.

THOMAS: You haven't.

SARAH: Does nobody listen to me? I said I taught Kitty to read just as you taught me.

THOMAS: Who knows this?

SARAH: Well you know it and I know it and Kitty knows it. It's not that difficult to learn to read, Thomas.

THOMAS: It's against the law.

SARAH: What is?

THOMAS: It's against the law to teach readin' and writin' to a slave!

SARAH: Don't be silly.

THOMAS: You've broken the law! You could go to jail! Papa could be fined a lotta money!

SARAH: I don't believe you.

THOMAS: Kitty'll have to be sold.

SARAH: No!

THOMAS: Yes she will, and all because a you! She'll be sold south and have to work in the fields!

SARAH: I didn't know!

THOMAS: You shoulda known.

SARAH: Nobody told me!

THOMAS: You coulda guessed.

SARAH: Well if I *had* known—

THOMAS: You'd have done it anyway!

SARAH: Yes I would!

THOMAS: Keep your voice down!

SARAH: *(Whispers.)* The institution a slavery is a sin and I will not be part of it!

THOMAS: You've broken the law a South Carolina!

SARAH: It's a criminal law.

THOMAS: You've placed Papa, and Kitty whom you profess to care for, in jeopardy!

SARAH: When I'm a lawyer I'll change such laws.

THOMAS: *(Laughs.)* What?

SARAH: I'll do away with slavery, I'll—

THOMAS: *(Laughing.)* What're you talkin' about now? Women can't be lawyers.

SARAH: Is there a law against that too?

THOMAS: Women can not be lawyers.

SARAH: I've taken Greek and Math and Latin and—

THOMAS: Papa allowed that only because I was bored by myself and it kept you quiet.

SARAH: I've studied legal codes just like you have and—

THOMAS: You're crazy.

SARAH: ... and Papa himself says I'll make the greatest jurist in the country!

THOMAS: That's a joke, he's makin' a joke!

SARAH: What's funny about it?!

THOMAS: Sarah, listen to me. There is no such thing as a woman lawyer.

SARAH: Why not?

THOMAS: It isn't right.

SARAH: Why's it right for you but not right for me?

THOMAS: What's right for you is wife and mother, that's God's plan.

SARAH: What about *my* plan?

THOMAS: You place yourself above God, do you?

SARAH: I'm only asking what my rights are in this matter.

THOMAS: You have the right to love and protection. Which you very well know.

SARAH: I don't want protection.

THOMAS: You may not want it but you need it.

SARAH: Why?

THOMAS: Well for one thing, you just say and do anything that comes into your head.

SARAH: What's wrong with that?

THOMAS: That's why Papa has to protect you and when you marry, your husband will protect you, and if he dies, your son, or I, I will protect you.

SARAH: No.

THOMAS: And with that protection comes your obligation to obey.

SARAH: Then I'm no better off than a slave.

THOMAS: And that's an example a the muddled thinkin' that proves just how much you need protectin'. You sat in on my classes and you didn't comprehend a thing.

SARAH: I comprehend what bein' a slave means! It means no education so a person can't defend herself, or earn a livin' or maintain an independent income, it means no controllin' the basic decisions a your life, and no legal recourse to right wrongs or injustices, that's what it means!

THOMAS: Shush up! You're actin' like a crazy person. Your hair is all over and your face is red and you sound like you should be locked up!

SARAH: I was just sayin'—

THOMAS: Shush. Do you want the whole house to hear?

SARAH: I—

THOMAS: We all love you, Sarah, that's what matters. Now ... sit down and be quiet and I promise I won't tell anybody about Kitty, but you have to promise to behave yourself.... Promise?

SARAH: If Greek and Latin and Law are denied me ... what can I study?

Scene Seven

WOMAN ONE: A little French

WOMAN THREE: and watercolour technique

WOMAN ONE: white on white embroidery
WOMAN THREE: and harpsichord lessons.

Scene Eight

SARAH: *(In her old age.)* I am deprived of an education.
WOMAN THREE: You may ride the chestnut gelding
SARAH: Yes.
WOMAN THREE: and sing a little.
SARAH: And sing a little.

Scene Nine

(MUSIC: Drums and chanting; continues underneath.)
WOMAN TWO: It is 1965. Anna Mae Pictou Aquash is a wife and mother of two children. Female children. In 1968 the American Indian Movement is founded. Anna Mae is living in Boston. She calls home on her twenty-fifth birthday, March 27th, 1970. Anna Mae is a Micmac. Anna Mae works with Indian people. Anna Mae cooks bannock. Teaches children. Is active in the Boston Indian Council. Is a ninth grade drop-out who is offered a scholarship to Brandeis University and turns it down because she is committed to the struggle for Native Rights. Anna Mae Pictou Aquash is divorced. Anna Mae Pictou Aquash. Is strong.

(SOUND: Interior of a car in motion; fades in and continues low underneath.)
WOMAN ONE: I didn't stop. Why should I stop? I felt as if it wouldn't be wise to stop. There were ten or twelve of them. White men. Just standing on the shoulder of the road, and as I passed, they stared at the car and I stared back. It was late in the afternoon. February 24th, 1976. It was about 4:30 in the afternoon, and a golden grey glow hung in the air. It was that time of year. And after I passed I stared in the rear-view mirror. I saw them staring back, watching the car disappear into the grey-gold luminescence. They no longer saw me yet I saw them, I saw them shift in the rear-view mirror, shift their ambiguous neutral gaze from the receding car to something on the shoulder of the road. It was red. Partly red. A red ... ski jacket perhaps ... or a bundle of red-coloured cloth. At their feet on the shoulder of the road. Something red.

(SOUND: Car grows faint.)

And I shifted my gaze from the rear-view mirror to the road ahead. I could see nothing ahead but the road and the jagged buttes of the Pine Ridge Reserve.

(MUSIC: Drums and chanting end.)

Scene Ten

(Parlour.)

ANGELINA: *(As a child. Off.)* Sarah! Sister Saaraaah!

THOMAS: It's Angelina.

(SOUND: Tea time; cups, saucers, pouring, stirring.)

ANGELINA: *(Off.)* Saaraaah!

SARAH: I hear her.

THOMAS: You're more mother than sister to her.

SARAH: I have replaced our own mother.

THOMAS: Why do you say that?

SARAH: Think about it, Thomas. Thirteen children in eighteen years?

THOMAS: *(Small laugh.)* Mother is just fine.

SARAH: A little tired, perhaps?

THOMAS: You imagine things. All I meant to say is that you're more than a sister to Angelina.

SARAH: I want her to grow secure in her own talents, independent, and courageous.

THOMAS: And so she is, you've seen to it.

SARAH: Yes, even as I grow more foolish.

THOMAS: Never you, Sarah.

SARAH: Oh yes. Fashionable, but foolish.

THOMAS: You're not unhappy.

SARAH: I grow weary of ballrooms, Thomas, and parlours.

THOMAS: Is it so bad?

SARAH: And every time I lift my eyes I am confronted by the face of slavery.

THOMAS: Marry, why don't you?

SARAH: *(A reaction of small amusement.)*

THOMAS: Come now, an honest question deserves an honest answer.

SARAH: Well then ... with marriage I fear I'd lose what small sense of self I still maintain.

THOMAS: The world is larger than Charleston. Marry wisely and well and you can see it.

SARAH: Is that the only way?

THOMAS: I'm afraid so.

SARAH: Then I'm afraid not.

ANGELINA: *(Off.)* Sister Saaraaah!

SARAH: *(Fading off.)* Yes Angelina, I'm coming, I'm on my way!

Scene Eleven

WOMAN TWO: In 1972 Anna Mae Pictou Aquash reads a brief item on Raymond Yellow Thunder in the Boston paper. Hundreds of thousands of Canadians and Americans read a brief item on Raymond Yellow Thunder in their papers. Raymond Yellow Thunder is a Sioux. In January 1972, Raymond Yellow Thunder is fifty-one years old. In February 1972, Raymond Yellow Thunder drinks too much in a bar. He is picked up by two white men, Melvin and Leslie Hare, who have drunk too much in a bar. Raymond Yellow Thunder is beaten, tortured, stripped naked and thrown on an American Legion dance floor. His body is found a week later in the trunk of a car. His relatives report it to the local police. They report it to the Bureau of Indian Affairs. They report it to the FBI. They get no response. The American Indian Movement is invited to the Pine Ridge Reserve to help clear up the case. Melvin and Leslie Hare will serve less than a year for the murder of Raymond Yellow Thunder. This kind of story is familiar to Anna Mae Pictou Aquash.

WOMAN THREE: In 1820, Sarah Moore Grimke was twenty-eight years old.

WOMAN TWO: In November 1972, the American Indian Movement's Trail of Broken Treaties' Caravan occupies the Bureau of Indian Affairs in Washington. Property is destroyed. Anna Mae Pictou Aquash is there.

Scene Twelve

(Parlour.)

SARAH: *(At age 28.)* I am convinced I have a gift for the ministry, Thomas.

THOMAS: You are always doin' one a two things, Sarah. You are deep in the midst of a whirl a fashionable social diversions, or you are announcin' every door a hope is closed and you have given over onto Death!

SARAH: I admit in the past I have veered between the two. Can't you understand I feel my life to be— [meaningless.]

THOMAS: *(Interrupting.)* And now—religious contemplation!

SARAH: This is an unmistakable call, Thomas, and not to be disregarded!

THOMAS: Why the Quakers?

SARAH: I must go north.

THOMAS: Ever since Father's death you've—

SARAH: Thomas.

THOMAS: You are an unmarried woman. An unmarried woman can live only with a family member, you— [know that.]

SARAH: I wish to live in Philadelphia ... with your permission.

THOMAS: What about Angelina?

SARAH: She's a young woman now. She must choose her own path as I've chosen mine.

THOMAS: You must—

SARAH: Thomas—

THOMAS: ... you must—

SARAH: Please.

THOMAS: ... go ... to Philadelphia and the Quakers then.

SARAH: *(Laughs joyfully.)* Oh Thomas. Thank you.

THOMAS: I must be mad.

SARAH: I am so happy.

(A moment of silence after the laughter.)

Scene Thirteen

(MUSIC: Drums and chanting; continues underneath.)

WOMAN TWO: The American Indian Movement is described as a small group of militants.

WOMAN ONE: The government says they do not represent the Reservation Indians of America.

WOMAN TWO: They say they are hoodlums

WOMAN ONE: criminals

WOMAN TWO: and in occupying the Bureau of Indian Affairs, and in the destruction of its property, they seek to obtain political objectives by replacing the democratic process with terrorist activity.

WOMAN ONE: Clyde Bellecourt of the American Indian Movement says: "The issue was, is, and forever will be, the occupation of Indian land, and the near destruction of a people by a nation of greedy and deceitful white men." Clyde Bellecourt says: "If you have any values higher than the possession of land, money and prestige, I would ask you to be outraged that your government values property more than human beings." Clyde Bellecourt says: "For every broken window in the Bureau of Indian Affairs there are a thousand broken hearts among our people which cannot be repaired."

(MUSIC: Ends.)

WOMAN TWO: Anna Mae Pictou Aquash agrees.

(MUSIC: Chord on harpsichord.)

Scene Fourteen

(Smaller parlour.)

ANGELINA: *(In her early 30s.)* It is 1834, Sarah, and absolutely nothin' is gonna change unless we take some action.

SARAH: *(At age 41.)* But ...

ANGELINA: I must speak out.

SARAH: Angelina ...

ANGELINA: I am forced to admit all my work at home does nothing to essentially change the abuses of slavery.

SARAH: I ...

ANGELINA: It's true. And I've watched your futile struggle for permission to speak as a minister, and I'll tell you and anybody else who cares to listen that Orthodox Quaker life is stultifyin' and soulquenchin' and all of your efforts have been as fruitless as mine.

SARAH: Shush.

ANGLINA: I will not shush. I've joined the Female Anti-Slavery Society of Philadelphia, and I've been asked to speak publicly on the evils of slavery and I intend to do so! *(Silence.)* Sarah? ... I hoped to do so with your blessing, Sarah. *(Silence.)*

SARAH: You know they say ... women are physically unable to speak loud enough to be heard in a public place.

ANGELINA: Do you believe that?

SARAH: Nooo ... they say—

ANGELINA: Who says?

SARAH: ... a woman's name should appear in print only thrice in her lifetime—

ANGELINA: At birth, marriage and death—and what do you say, Sarah? Speak.

SARAH: I say ... I say, how can I help?

ANGELINA: *(Laughs.)* I knew it.

SARAH: You'll need someone to organize things.

ANGELINA: To accompany me, for there'll be touring.

SARAH: *(Laughs.)* And all my years a study will not be in vain. You can speak a the false interpretation a the Bible to justify slavery, and the twists and turns the law must take to uphold an institution that has no legal basis!

ANGELINA: Not me. I'll speak a what I've seen myself—the slave's life in the fields, the house and on the block.

SARAH: You're right.

ANGELINA: And *you* must speak a what *you* know.

SARAH: I can't.

ANGELINA: If I can you can.

SARAH: I'm forty-one years old, Angelina. I don't know if I have anything worth saying.

ANGELINA: That isn't true.

SARAH: I know I have this fear.

ANGELINA: You gave me courage as a child. Now I return it.

SARAH: I ...

ANGELINA: Take courage, Sarah.

SARAH: I ... I will speak, and ... and ... on the equality a women as well for there's a similarity between the law as it pertains to women and to Blacks, and I will speak it!

(SOUND: Clatter of telegraph.)

Scene Fifteen

WOMAN TWO: In November and December 1972, Oglala Sioux on the Pine Ridge Reserve attempt to impeach their tribal chairman Richard Wilson. In February 1973, Wilson mounts a machine gun on the reserve office roof, and surrounds himself with seventy-five armed marshalls, in addition to his squad of personal bodyguards some call goons. Wilson himself chairs a third hearing into graft and corruption charges laid against himself by the Oglala Sioux Civil Rights Organization. He finds himself not guilty. Men from the Bureau of Indian Affairs, the FBI and the Marshalls' Service, with logistical support from the Pentagon, arrive on the reserve to impose the will of Richard Wilson on Pine Ridge residents. With legal channels blocked, Sioux Elders, young traditionalists and the Oglala Sioux Civil Rights Organization request the advice and assistance of the American Indian Movement. On February 27th, 1973, supporters of Oglala Sioux Civil Rights and the American Indian Movement begin a seventy-one-day occupation of the village of Wounded Knee to voice their protest. They are surrounded by government forces.

(SOUND: Faint church bells toll.)

In Boston, Anna Mae Pictou Aquash calls home on March 27th, her twenty-eighth birthday. In April she and her second husband-to-be, Nogeeshik, drive a van-load of supplies over back roads into Wounded Knee. Anna Mae digs bunkers. Anna Mae patrols the camp's perimeter at night. She is calm. She makes jokes as government gunfire riddles the village. She misses her two girls who are with their father in Nova Scotia. It is too dangerous for them to be with her. In her hair, Anna Mae ties a red ribbon.

Scene Sixteen

(Meeting place, small church.)
(SOUND: Applause and murmur of voices.)
ANGELINA: *(Over noise.)* Thank you ladies and gentlemen—and now my sister, Sarah Moore Grimke!
(SOUND: Applause; continues underneath a bit of SARAH's speech.)
SARAH: *(Fading on over applause; we are picking up speech in midstream.)* Women are bought and sold in our slave markets to satisfy the brutal lust of those who bear the names of Christians! If a Black woman desires to preserve her virtue, she is either bribed or whipped into compliance! If she dares to resist her seducer, her life, by the laws of some states, may be and has been sacrificed to the fury of disappointed passion! Can any woman hear of such things, and then sit back, fold her hands and say, "I have nothing to do with this"?
WOMAN TWO: Frank Clearwater is an Apache.
SARAH: No, she cannot and be guiltless!

Scene Seventeen

WOMAN TWO: On April 17th, 1973, while sleeping in the Wounded Knee Catholic Church, Frank Clearwater is hit by government M-16 gunfire. Frank Clearwater dies on April 27th, 1973. Buddy Lamont is an Oglala Sioux. On April 26th, Buddy Lamont is hit by an M-16 at 8:30 a.m. At 11:30 a.m. government forces allow a Sioux medic to approach him to render medical aid. Buddy Lamont is dead. On May 8th, 1973, a ceasefire is negotiated. The government promises a treaty commission and investigation of tribal chairman Richard Wilson's administration.
WOMAN THREE: In 1837, Sarah Grimke publishes *Letters on the Equality of the Sexes*. Both content and title are condemned as heresy.
WOMAN TWO: The commission effects no change. Anna Mae is not surprised.

Scene Eighteen

(Church pulpit.)
MALE VOICE: When woman assumes the place and tone of man as a public reformer, our care and protection of her seem unnecessary, and

her character becomes unnatural, for if the vine, whose strength and beauty is to lean upon the trellis and half conceal its clusters, thinks to assume the independence and overshadowing nature of the elm, it will not only cease to bear fruit, but will fall in dishonour into the dust!

Scene Nineteen

WOMAN TWO: Richard Wilson continues as chairman of the tribal council. His goon squad continues to enforce his will on the Pine Ridge Reserve. Anna Mae is not surprised.

Scene Twenty

(Town meeting-hall.)

SARAH: I ask no favours for my sex! I surrender not our claim to equality! All I ask of our brethren is that they take their feet from off our necks so we may stand upright on that ground which God designed us to occupy.

Scene Twenty-One

WOMAN TWO: The federal government arrests 560 Indians and non-Indians on charges related to the occupation of Wounded Knee. Interstate and other arrests bring the number to 1200. Anna Mae Pictou Aquash faces minor charges. Subsequent trials will reveal government misdeeds, perjured testimony, fabricated evidence and illegal surveillance. By 1976, virtually every leader of the American Indian Movement will be in jail, driven underground, or dead.

Scene Twenty-Two

(Parlour.)
(MUSIC: Chord on harpsichord.)
SARAH: Tea, Mr. Weld?
WELD: Thank you, ma'am.
(SOUND: Cup, saucer, pouring, stirring, drinking.)
ANGELINA: Sarah?
SARAH: Please.
ANGELINA: More cake, Mr. Weld?
WELD: It *is* delicious, ma'am.

ANGELINA: Sarah?

SARAH: I ... don't think so, thank you, Angelina.

ANGELINA: This is somewhat of a special day.

SARAH: Yes indeed.

WELD: Your sister means a great deal to me, Miss Grimke.

SARAH: I'm happy for you, for both of you. Angelina's happiness means a great deal to me.

ANGELINA: And Sarah does so admire your work on behalf of the anti-slavery movement, Mr. Weld. Don't you, Sarah?

SARAH: Oh yes. Although I must confess, in the area of women's rights I find— [little to reassure me.]

WELD: Aaaah Miss Grimke—Sarah if I may—one issue at a time. And women's rights is not a life and death issue.

SARAH: So you say.

WELD: We must act against slavery now.

SARAH: I don't see that acting on one negates acting on t'other. To the contrary—

ANGELINA: Do try the cake, Sarah.

WELD: No muzzling of your sister, Angelina. She must speak what she feels.

SARAH: I believe I will have some cake ... thank you.

ANGELINA: Did you know that in Mr. Weld's—

WELD: Theodore please.

ANGELINA: Theodore's ministry, he allows women to speak at revivals?

SARAH: Allows?

ANGELINA: *(Whispers.)* Shush.

SARAH: *(Whispers.)* Well I don't think that "allows" quite does it.

WELD: Today is a happy day. Today we speak of the union of Angelina and myself; all other issues, even slavery, must wait until tomorrow.

SARAH: Maybe so ... maybe so.

Scene Twenty-Three

WOMAN TWO: It is 1974. Anna Mae and Nogeeshik separate. She works full time for the American Indian Movement in St. Paul, Minneapolis. She is a spiritual person who inspires others.

Scene Twenty-Four

(Inside car.)

(SOUND: Car in motion; fades under speech and out at end.)

WOMAN ONE: I didn't stop. I kept on driving. Although it seemed as if I slowed down. I might have slowed down. I might have gone slower. It wasn't that cold, although it was late in the afternoon. It was about 4:30. There were ten or twelve of them. They were alone. I don't know how they got there. I didn't see any means of transportation, any way for them to get there. They were just there. And they didn't do anything. They weren't doing anything. They were standing there, and they stared at the car as I drove by. They stared until they shifted in my rear-view mirror, and then they looked down. At the ground. Something on the ground. I think it was red. I thought of turning around and driving back. Passing them again. But I didn't. I thought that if I did, they might not be there. They'd be gone, they wouldn't be there. Or else they would. Be there. So I didn't. I drove on. Towards Route 90. And off the Pine Ridge Reserve.

Scene Twenty-Five

(Music room.)

(MUSIC: Harpsichord, with mistakes, as opposed to chords or scales; continues underneath.)

SARAH: Stop.... We have to talk, Angelina ... will you please stop?

ANGELINA: I come to it late and I shall never improve if I don't practice.

SARAH: What does it matter?

ANGELINA: Theodore loves the harpsichord.

SARAH: Well then let him play it.

ANGELINA: Shush.

SARAH: I'm sorry, but we must talk.

ANGELINA: Alright.

(SOUND: Harpsichord out. Silence.)

Well?

SARAH: I ...

ANGELINA: Speak.

SARAH: Do you know that Theodore has spoken to me.

ANGELINA: He's tryin' to be helpful.

SARAH: You told him then.

ANGELINA: He is my husband, Sarah.

SARAH: I know.

ANGELINA: I didn't think it was a secret, at least you never said so.

SARAH: I know. I thought ...

ANGELINA: I simply mentioned, in a general sort of way, your great lack of confidence as regards your speaking abilities, and Theodore, in a spirit of brotherhood and love, thought you would accept his comments in the spirit in which he offered them.

SARAH: His kindest words concern my delivery which he says is wooden, monotonous and heavy, weakening rather than increasing the power of truth.

ANGELINA: Directness is Theodore's forte, and an essential facet of his teaching.

SARAH: But why has no one else ever spoken of this?

ANGELINA: Who knows, it may be a matter of standards, or—

SARAH: Do you think me so inept?

ANGELINA: I ... you know domestic duties I ... when did we last share a platform?

SARAH: And then, was I effective then?

ANGELINA: Theodore—

SARAH: Do I harm the cause rather than advancing it?

(SOUND: A baby cries faintly; continues underneath.)

ANGELINA: *(Fading off.)* I don't know, Sarah. I think it wise to at least consider Theodore's words.... *(To the baby.)* There, there ... he means well ... there ...

(SOUND: Baby cries end.)

SARAH: *(To herself.)* Why has no one else mentioned this? Oh I ... I ...

Scene Twenty-Six

(Collage.)

WOMAN THREE: Sarah Moore Grimke accepted no more public-speaking engagements and ceased her writing on women's rights.

WOMAN TWO: In 1974, at the Red School House in St. Paul, Anna Mae Pictou Aquash dreams a dream of compiling a comprehensive cultural history of Native people in Canada and the United States, cross-referencing oral and traditional research sources. She works to implement it with Native students.

WELD: Your place is with us, Sarah. Our home is your home. Angelina needs you and I can deny my wife nothing.

WOMAN TWO: In August 1974, Ojibway Warriors occupy Anicinabe Park near Kenora, Ontario. Anna Mae is there.

WELD: Angelina is weakened by childbirth, Sarah. Dr. Wilson says her nervous system is quite simply shattered. Without you overseeing domestic duties in the house I don't know how we'd manage.

WOMAN TWO: During 1974 Anna Mae organizes the American Indian Movement's Los Angeles office into an effective fund-raising operation.

WELD: Have not these last two decades brought you joy and peace, Sarah? When I think of your previous years, the speeches, the pamphleteering, equality this, legality that ...

WOMAN TWO: January 1st, 1975. The Menominee Warriors occupy the Alexian Brothers' Monastery on disputed Menominee land. Anna Mae is there.

WELD: I tell you, when Angelina first introduced us, I thought what manner of woman—if woman it be—is this?

WOMAN TWO: June 26th, 1975. Two FBI agents are shot to death taking part in a raid on Jumping Bull's residence on the Pine Ridge Reserve. The FBI says it is an action initiated to serve a warrant, which it turns out has not been issued, on a young man who it turns out is not present. Some say the agents are killed in crossfire; some say by FBI fire. Anna Mae Pictou Aquash is not there. She is in Cedar Rapids, Iowa, speaking to a citizens' group.

WELD: As I have so often said to Angelina, heaven has appointed to one sex the superior, and to the other, the subordinate role ...

WOMAN TWO: September 3rd, 1975. The FBI raid the home of spiritual leader Leonard Crow Dog. Anna Mae Pictou Aquash is there. She is arrested, stripped, searched and interrogated.

WELD: And the moment woman begins to feel the promptings of ambition or the thirst for power, her aegis of defence is gone.

WOMAN TWO: Anna Mae Pictou Aquash is threatened with serious felony charges. She denies them. Anna Mae Pictou Aquash is accused of witnessing the FBI agents' deaths at the Jumping Bull raid. She denies it. Anna Mae Pictou Aquash is offered a deal. In return for information to be used in locating and convicting American Indian Movement's leaders of murder in the death of the agents, all charges against her will be dropped. Anna Mae refuses. She is released on bail.

Scene Twenty-Seven

(Small parlour.)

SARAH: *(In her 70s. Hums a soft, rather tuneless hum.)*

ANGELINA: *(In her 60s.)* What're you readin'?

SARAH: Pardon?

ANGELINA: I said, what're you readin', Sarah?

SARAH: Studying.

(SOUND: Pages turn.)

ANGELINA: Pardon?

SARAH: I am studyin', Angelina. I am studyin' French.

ANGELINA: *(Small laugh.)* But what on earth for?

SARAH: For reasons a my own.

ANGELINA: You're over seventy, Sarah.

SARAH: I can count, and all the more reason to get to it now before it's too late.

ANGELINA: Get to what?

SARAH: I've decided to translate Lamartine's biography of Joan of Arc. I believe women and men have a need to know more a this woman a great courage, this female leader a men! And I intend to introduce them to her! But first—I must master French.

Scene Twenty-Eight

WOMAN THREE: Sarah Grimke's translation of Lamartine's *Joan of Arc* was published in 1868.

WOMAN TWO: October 1975. Anna Mae Pictou Aquash is informed of her trial date. The information is erroneous, or the date is changed without informing Anna Mae or her counsel. When she fails to appear, a warrant is issued for her arrest. November 1975. Anna Mae is arrested in Oregon and transported in chains to South Dakota. Anna Mae expresses a fear for her life if she fails to comply with the FBI's request for information in exchange for the dropping of charges.

Scene Twenty-Nine

(Small parlour.)

SARAH: *(At age 75. Hums a soft tuneless hum.)*

ANGELINA: *(In her 60s.)* What're you writin', Sarah?

SARAH: I've read a most interestin' book.

ANGELINA: Oh?

SARAH: *The Subjection of Women* by John Stuart Mill.

ANGELINA: Really?

SARAH: Really. And I've decided to request permission to act as Mr. Mill's agent in Massachusetts for the book's distribution. I believe it's important.

ANGELINA: Have you gone mad?

SARAH: Most probably.

ANGELINA: And how do you intend to distribute it?

SARAH: I'll sell it door to door.

ANGELINA: Personally?

SARAH: A course personally.

ANGELINA: *(Clears her throat.)* You're a woman a some years, Sarah.

SARAH: I am that.

ANGELINA: Be reasonable.

SARAH: I am seventy-five to be precise, and I've been "reasonable" long enough. And should any profit ensue from my sales of Mr. Mill's most interestin' book, I shall donate it to the journal.

ANGELINA: The one on women's suffrage?

SARAH: Correct, Angelina, Women's Suffrage!

Scene Thirty

WOMAN TWO: November 24th, 1975. Anna Mae is released in the custody of her lawyer until her trial on the 25th. On the night of the 24th, Anna Mae steps out of a hotel room into a car and heads west.

A bench warrant is issued for her arrest, followed by a ten-count indictment arising from her Oregon arrest.

Scene Thirty-One

(Hall.)

(SOUND: Winter storm and wind. Door opens, storm up.)

ANGELINA: *(In her old age.)* Sarah! Where're you going?!

SARAH: *(In her old age. Off.)* Into town and about!

ANGELINA: On foot in this weather?

SARAH: *(Off.)* I must have more signatures for the vote!

ANGELINA: Not today, Sarah.

SARAH: *(Off.)* I confess it's not pleasant work—and one's often subjected to rudeness as well as the cold but *(Fading off.)* it's a fight worth fighting. I'll see you at dinner.

(SOUND: Door closes. Storm down.)

ANGELINA: *(Low voice.)* Mercy me.

WOMAN TWO: During 1975 the murder rate on the Pine Ridge Reserve is higher than in the city of Chicago. Most of the victims are American Indian Movement leaders or supporters.

ANGELINA: *(Low voice.)* Mercy mercy me.

Scene Thirty-Two

(Inside car.)

(SOUND: Interior of car in motion; fading underneath.)

WOMAN TWO: South Dakota Senator James Abourez states: "The Pine Ridge Reserve is being run like Hitler's Germany."

WOMAN ONE: It is February 24th, 1976.

WOMAN TWO: Some people believe the FBI allows Anna Mae to escape in the hope she will lead them to leaders of the American Indian Movement who have fled underground.

WOMAN ONE: It is thirty days before Anna Mae's thirty-first birthday.

WOMAN TWO: Some people believe the FBI generates a rumour that Anna Mae is an informer to pressure her into informing.

WOMAN ONE: I drive through the Pine Ridge Reserve in South Dakota on my way to Route 90.

(MUSIC: Drums, chanting.)

WOMAN TWO: Some people believe a systematic campaign of harassment and intimidation is carried out against Anna Mae Pictou Aquash by the FBI, the objective of which is her testimony, perjured or otherwise, against the leaders of the American Indian Movement.

WOMAN ONE: Near Wanblee I pass a group of men. White men. About ten or twelve of them standing by the side of the road.

WOMAN TWO: An FBI summary of the interrogation of Anna Mae Pictou Aquash reports her statement to agent David Price. "You can either shoot me or throw me in jail as those are the only two choices I'm making."

WOMAN ONE: They stare at the car as I drive by.

WOMAN TWO: Anna Mae alleges her life is threatened by agent Price.

WOMAN ONE: In the rear-view mirror I see something on the ground at their feet.

WOMAN TWO: His words are reported as: "You cooperate and live. You don't cooperate and die."

WOMAN ONE: Something red ... a small bundle, or jacket perhaps.

WOMAN TWO: December 25th, 1975. Anna Mae Pictou Aquash does not call home.

WOMAN ONE: I don't stop.

WOMAN TWO: Nor will she call home on March 27th, 1976, her thirty-first birthday.

WOMAN ONE: I continue on.

WOMAN TWO: On February 24th, 1976, the body of a Native woman is found at the foot of an embankment near Wanblee on the Pine Ridge Reserve in South Dakota. Some people are surprised at the number of lawmen who converge at the death site of this unknown Native.

WOMAN ONE: But I remember them, standing there, ten or twelve white men on the shoulder of the road on the Pine Ridge Reserve—

WOMAN TWO: Representing the FBI, the Bureau of Indian Affairs, the local county sheriff office and its deputies. The body lies on its left side, knees drawn up, wearing jeans, sneakers, a light shirt, a red ski jacket and carrying no identification. FBI agent David Price takes a number of photographs. He fails to identify the body.

(MUSIC: Ends.)

WOMAN ONE: The moment sticks.

(*SOUND: Interior of car in motion; fades out and is gone by the end of the following speech.*)

WOMAN TWO: The Bureau of Indian Affairs' autopsy report states cause of death as exposure. The hands are severed for the purpose of identification. The body is buried in an unmarked grave.

WOMAN ONE: On March 6th, 1976, the body of an unknown Native woman found near Wanblee of the Pine Ridge Reserve on February 24th is identified by fingerprints as that of Anna Mae Pictou Aquash from the Micmac Reserve near Shubenacadie, Nova Scotia.

WOMAN TWO: Anna Mae's body is exhumed for a second autopsy at the request of family members and the American Indian Movement's lawyers.

WOMAN ONE: There is dried blood in her hair. There is a visible bulge of her left temple.

WOMAN TWO: There is a bullet hole in the base of her skull behind her right ear. The death of Anna Mae Pictou Aquash is the result of a gun being fired at close range into her head. The bullet is lodged in her left temple.

WOMAN ONE: Her hair clasp is found on the top of the embankment near the shoulder of the road near Wanblee on the Pine Ridge Reserve.

WOMAN TWO: Some people say Anna Mae Pictou Aquash would have been a key witness countering government charges against the leaders of the American Indian Movement.

WOMAN ONE: Some people say the killing is an execution-style slaying.

WOMAN TWO: Some people say the authorities' handling of the case is curious.

WOMAN ONE: Some people say the conduct of the FBI raises serious questions.

WOMAN TWO: At the urging of numerous organizations representing church, civil, legal, women and Native rights groups, the Canadian government says it will ask Washington about it.

WOMAN ONE: June 29th, 1976. External Affairs Minister Allen MacEachern produces a FBI press release in response to queries in the House of Commons. It is a media statement acknowledging the discovery of her body. Anna Mae Pictou Aquash would not be surprised.

WOMAN TWO: October 1976. In response to further queries in the House of Commons, External Affairs Minister Don Jamieson produces an FBI press release identical to the media statement of June 29th, updated by two additional paragraphs acknowledging lack of progress in the case. Anna Mae Pictou Aquash would not be surprised.

WOMAN ONE: The Aquash affair soon slips into oblivion. It is heard of no more.

WOMAN TWO: That is, not in the House of Commons.

(SOUND: Bells ringing in House of Commons.)

Scene Thirty-Three

(Collage.)

SARAH: *(At age 78.)* It's me.

WOMAN ONE: Anna Mae Pictou Aquash is not forgotten.

SARAH: It's Sarah. Sarah Moore Grimke. And it's snowin' today. Snowin' hard.

WOMAN TWO: We have not forgotten.

SARAH: I don't much fancy goin' out in it, but I intend to. Yes I do. I intend to test the legality a denyin' the vote to women. Today I intend to present myself at the pollin' booth. In order to vote. And they'll deny me. But I do intend doin' that, and continuin' to do that till the day I die. *(Chuckles.)* Yes I do. If I can get there in this weather. That's what I'm doin' today. And it oughta set them right on their ear!

WOMAN ONE: And tomorrow?

WOMAN TWO: Tomorrow.

SARAH: You know I'm seventy-eight years old, and some people say this struggle will be the death a me. Some people say I should cease my efforts, for those who stand against us are strong. But I say I am a free agent

WOMAN ONE: gifted with intelligence

WOMAN TWO: and endowed with immortality!

Scene Thirty-Four

(Outside car.)

(SOUND: Stationary car, engine running; fades in.)

WOMAN ONE: Are you coming?

SARAH: *(At age 78.)* And I will not cease. Not till the day I die. *(Chuckles.)* Not even then.

WOMAN TWO: Get in.

SARAH: And I urge my sisters to lay aside the traditions of men as well as their prejudices and join me in examinin' subjects for ourselves, and in actin' on what we discover!

WOMAN ONE: Come on.

WOMAN THREE: Sarah Moore Grimke died in 1873 at the age of eighty-one.

WOMAN TWO: Anna Mae Pictou Aquash lives.

WOMAN ONE: We won't forget.

(SOUND: Car door shuts.)

WOMAN TWO: Nor the struggle cease.

(SOUND: Car door shuts.)

Scene Thirty-Five

(Inside car.)

WOMAN THREE: Remember

WOMAN ONE: remember

WOMAN TWO: remember

(SOUND: Car pulls away, fades into distance. Silence.)

That's Extraordinary!

by Diana Raznovich

translated by
Rosalind Goldsmith

DIANA RAZNOVICH seems truly surprised when asked if she writes anything other than comedies. The playwright, novelist, poet and cartoonist looks puzzled as the interpreter explains, then replies, "What else exists besides comedy? I see life as very, very funny." But after describing one of her plays, *Casa Matriz*, in which women can rent mean or loving mothers by the day, she mentions that she hopes people will laugh *and* cry as the play ends. "This is my cruel intention, to make them do both. I want people to start laughing, but a few minutes later to ask themselves, 'What am I laughing about? This is *awful*.'"

Raznovich has described humour as "a rupture, a transgression of how life is supposed to be.... At the same time humour is tied to pleasure because it produces laughter, and when people laugh, they feel positively connected with something and they understand it better because they've enjoyed it." The world is not lacking in targets for Raznovich's wit. One of her favourite topics is media excess and exploitation, another is the sophisticated consumerism she satirizes in *Casa Matriz* and other plays. One of her plays, *Jardín Otoño* (Autumn Garden) has two elderly women kidnap the adored star of a soap opera, then return the actor when they realize he is less fascinating than his on-screen persona. Although in this play and others she bursts the balloon of women's fantasies, Raznovich is quick to point out that men also buy into media myths, especially the sales pitch that "someone will save you. It's not only women. Everyone expects to be saved."

That's Extraordinary! was written expressly for Morningside Drama, though Raznovich says it can be understood wherever people turn on radios or televisions. "I didn't want to give it a specific geographical setting," she says of the play. "But I feel that it's a big urban setting, that it has an American style. A woman who has decided to commit suicide has to leave the city to find the countryside where she can do it, but she discovers that the radio is using her suicide. It could be any European country or American, or Argentina. Sensationalism with death exists everywhere.

"The pornographic display of the Gulf War happened everywhere. Though it was American-orchestrated, it really was the media of all the world. And the Kurdish genocide is transmitted exactly the same way, with takes of people dying of hunger and children being buried. I think producing those sensationalist programs is extraordinarily more expensive than feeding those people, and yet the media prefers to spend the money on producing those programs instead of finding a way to relieve the tragedy."

Raznovich says she chose to focus on only one woman, who could be anyone in an urban, middle-class setting. "I thought I should address the listener more directly and allow the average audience member to identify with that person, rather than a Kurdish mass, which they consider a faceless other," she says. "Alicia is someone just like you, just like me."

At first, it does seem that Alicia may have a rescuer. But the star reporter who interrupts the suicide attempt turns out to be just another twist in Alicia's troubles. "Not only doesn't he save her, he says to her that *she* has to save *him*, that he's a poor journalist without a job," says Raznovich. "She's going to die anyway, so would she be so kind as to give him her last words so that he can sell them." What stops Alicia from pulling the trigger on herself is her realization that she has been invaded by the media and her resulting rage.

"She has an accidental discovery: by interviewing someone just before they kill themselves you can stop them from wanting to commit suicide. So she is saved at the end, but she gets saved because she penetrates a more lucid zone, where she can see what she's being used for. It's not nature that saves her, but her anger at being used," says Raznovich. In the first draft, Raznovich had Alicia actually kill the reporter, but the final version leaves the drama a little more open-ended.

Combining rage with humour is second nature to Raznovich—as she puts it, "I live this." She is the third generation in a Jewish family to have left "home" country. Her father's family emigrated from Russia because of anti-Semitic pogroms; her mother's family fled Vienna because of Hitler. Raznovich left Argentina's dictatorship behind in 1976. Although she now considers Spain home, she credits Argentina, specifically Argentinian theatre, for introducing her to the power of the imagination.

"It was an interesting era in the theatre in Argentina," she says. "I was raised in a very stimulating environment. Buenos Aires was a very creative city, there was always a lot to do in the theatre. There was very little money, but a lot of imagination and ideas. That was useful for me for Europe because in Europe, it is exactly the opposite—a lot of money and very few ideas."

Radio drama is another thing Raznovich finds "very funny." "It's very interesting to be blind, not to see, only to hear," she says. "I love music very much and it's a very interesting experience not to see an image. We are saturated by visual images—this is the era of visual images and it's as if we are absent from our own images. To produce only for the ear triggers ambiguity—everything can have one face or another, one colour or another, one style or another. Radio makes the entire audience seem as blind people who are just enjoying themselves through the ears. The challenge is to produce through the ears, through hearing, all of the sensations that can be produced otherwise with visual images."

Raznovich says she is fascinated by her plays' receptions in other countries, thrilled that her stories and sense of humour translate. "I don't believe in nations but in the whole earth, the whole world," she says. "I feel that we have to take possession of the entire planet and live as one. Artists work with feelings and essentially all people resemble each other very much.

"The place where I was most worried about my work was Germany, because I thought German people were very serious and wouldn't laugh at my kind of humour. I was very surprised at the warm welcome my work had there. I said, well, people are all the same. They laugh about the same things, and feelings are really universal."

Certainly the main themes in Raznovich's writing, which she describes as "life and dying," are universal.

What words would she like on her own tombstone?

"Don't worry, be happy."

DIANA RAZNOVICH was born in Buenos Aires, Argentina in 1945 and has been living in Madrid, Spain since 1976. She describes herself as a typical, nomadic Jew. She has published three books of poetry, *Tiempo de amar*, *Caminata en tu sombra* and *De personajes altos imposibles*. Her novels include *Para que se cumplan todos tus deseos*, *El Ejército Hueco*, *Mater Erótica* and *Top-Model*. She is a cartoonist, and had a weekly assignment for the newspaper *Tiempo Argentino* for four years. Her biting humour shows up in her more than twenty plays, which include *Buscapies*, *Plaza Hay una sola*, *El Guardagente*, *El desconcierto*, *Jardín de Otoño*, *Efectos Personales* and *Casa Matriz*. They have been staged in Spain and other countries, in particular Argentina, Brazil, Paraguay, Italy, Germany and France. She recently wrote a musical comedy about Christopher Columbus. She has also written radio dramas, many of which have been produced in Germany, and scripts for the television series *Barbara Narvaez*, which was widely broadcast by Latin-American networks.

ROSALIND GOLDSMITH was born in England in 1956, and grew up in Canada. She trained as an actor in England while living there from 1979 to 1984. Her radio dramas include *The Favourite*, produced for Stereo Theatre in 1986 and a prize-winner at the International Radio Festival of New York and *Miguel*, aired on Stereo Theatre in 1987. *Off the Agenda*, produced for Morningside Drama in 1988, led to her documentary on East Timor for CBC's documentary program Ideas the same year. In 1990, she wrote her first stage play, *Who's There?* Her most recent work for radio is *The London Tapes*.

Characters

ALICIA early forties
GASPAR radio journalist, late twenties
MC broadcaster, deep, rich voice

Production Credits

That's Extraordinary! was commissioned by the Canadian Broadcasting Corporation for Morningside Drama and first broadcast on the CBC Radio network on May 17, 1991.

ALICIA Valerie Pearson
GASPAR Jeff Haslam
MC Earl Klein

Produced and directed in Edmonton by Kathleen Flaherty. Recording Engineer: Al Lamden. Sound effects by Eric Wagers. Sound Consultant: Marcel Hamel. Production Assistant: Ivan Todosijczuk. Script Editor: Dave Carley. Executive Producer of Morningside Drama: James Roy.

That's Extraordinary!

Scene One

(*SOUND: ALICIA walks, autumn leaves crackling under her feet. She pants as she climbs a hill. Wind in the tops of the trees. ALICIA stops.*)

ALICIA: (*Inhales the fresh morning air.*) It's nice here. Deserted. This is a good place to say goodbye to the world. Dawn. The rocks look black. The sky so dark and full of clouds. It seems somehow right for me to die under this stormy sky. (*Sings softly, sadly.*) Goodbye beautiful clouds! We won't see each other again.... (*Pulls herself up.*) Come on, let's not be gloomy at the last minute. (*Tries to be brave.*) I'll die laughing! (*Laughs, tries to be cheerful, stops short. Admits to herself.*) But ... I'm afraid. That's the truth. Those trees have turned their backs on me. They're hiding, and even the flowers shiver when they see my gun....

(*SOUND: She loads the gun.*)

I'm trembling like you, my dear, beautiful red poppies!

(*SOUND: She plays with the gun, loading it and unloading it.*)

(*Laughs anxiously.*) It's not easy to be the criminal and the victim at the same time! My own executioner ... Alicia's obedient assassin: Alicia. (*Breathes.*) I must climb higher.

(*SOUND: Stronger wind. ALICIA climbs. She stumbles into an enormous rock, sits on it.*)

(*Out of breath.*) From up here my own life seems so far away, like someone else's story. (*Sighs.*) Pitiful story. At least it could do with a dignified ending.

(*SOUND: All nature seems to unleash itself. The trees creak and stir in the wind. Dry leaves blown everywhere; continues underneath.*)

How much time I've lost in lost causes! I don't blame anybody ... no. They won't even notice when I've gone, since they never noticed me when I was there. (*With irony.*) Someone will say: Miss Alicia didn't come today. Today she didn't cross the blue bridge clutching all her papers. Today she didn't eat alone at Joseph's restaurant. Today she didn't talk to her mirror. Today she didn't stay stuck to the telephone waiting for him to call. Today she has missed all her appointments. *(Overcome.)* Today ...

(SOUND: Wind howls furiously, swish of leaves.)

(Speaks to the wind, her voice battling against the gale.) Blow wind! Come on, blow! Take away all my fear! Take away my love—the love I gave to Peter that he never gave to me! Blow white wind and fill me with your rage, your power! Give me all the strength I need to pull this trigger! *(Decided.)* I'll count to three and then I'll do it. Then it will all be over for me. One ... two ... two ... two and ... two and ... One, two and— *(Furious with herself.)* I can't! I can't!

(SOUND: Wind drops. Calms. A gentle breeze, becoming more and more distant. A few birds chirp.)

And now the wind has stopped! And the sun! The sun's coming out! *(Daunted, frightened.)* How am I going to have the courage to say goodbye to the rest of my days in front of that beautiful sun? Oh God! Why do you make things even more difficult for me? Give me back my storm!

Scene Two

(MUSIC: Theme music of the radio program "That's Extraordinary!"—a catchy upbeat tune breaking the mood of the previous scene.)

MC: *(Professional, enthusiastic, false voice.)* Good morning, ladies and gentlemen! And welcome to another morning with your friendly radio! Stay with us for "That's Extraordinary!" The hottest radio program on the international airwaves! *(With the same demagogic tone.)* As always, at your service to bring direct into your home: life itself! And so ... *(Emphatic, inquisitive.)* Isn't death just one side, one facet, we might say, of life?

(MUSIC: Suspenseful.)

Because we believe that death is an intimate part of life, we are bringing to you today, direct, live and on location, an actual suicide.

(MUSIC: Well-known march.)

Yes, ladies and gentlemen! The extraordinary and more and more extraordinary! Today we present "Suicide on a Hilltop."

(MUSIC: March.)

What you have just heard was the fantastic but real testimony of a woman about to kill herself, captured by our secret microphones, especially arranged so that you can enjoy listening to a real suicide in the comfort of your own home.

(MUSIC: Suspenseful.)

(In a salesman tone, with professional pride.) Our program has stopped at nothing. We've been following Miss "A" for the last eight days, since the time we knew she had decided to take her own life. And now we can present to you, live and direct into your own home: her final words.

(MUSIC: Chords of triumphal march music between each of the following words.)

Unique! Unrepeatable! Shocking!

(MUSIC: Suspenseful; builds underneath.)

(Speaks invitingly, as if to each listener.) She, of course, has no idea about our extraordinary report today. She doesn't know that her final words are being transmitted to thousands and thousands of eager radio listeners. Neither does she know that we have sent our own intrepid reporter, Gaspar Wolf, to the scene to interview her live and on location. Hello Gaspar? Are you there?

Scene Three

GASPAR: *(Enthusiastic, close on.)* Good morning, William. I'm here, hidden behind some shrubs, and from my vantage point I can see today's interviewee quite clearly—in fact, she's only about a stone's throw away.

MC: We have heard directly her conversations with the wind, the poppies, the sun and God, and I must say it has been stupendous to follow her final emotions at such close range. But our curiosity has no end. Tell us—what does she look like?

GASPAR: *(Syrupy.)* She ... what does she look like? She's ... tall, fair, blue eyes. She's very pale, really ... not of this world, white as a sheet.... She's been lifting the gun to her head and then ... pulling it back. She's wearing a charming suit of autumn shades, she's a woman of about forty.... Oh, she has an air about her ... she's a classic beauty.... But hang on—she's moving her lips, she's ... *(Stops himself. ALICIA has done something unexpected.)* Oh!! No!! No!! You can't imagine what I'm seeing, my God! Just a minute! She's lifted the gun to her head with more conviction this time. *(Enthused.)* She seems totally decided!! Here we go! She's going to do it!!!

(MUSIC: Suspenseful. Drum roll.)

MC: *(Low, intense, like a golf commentator.)* You are listening to "That's Extraordinary!"—the program with an impact! And for those of you who may have just joined us, "That's Extraordinary!" presents to you today a person just like yourself or myself, a person who, within a few precious moments, will actually cross over that barrier that separates life from death.

(MUSIC: Triumphal march; continues underneath.)

Stay tuned! Don't lose a second! Every second could be the last!

Scene Four

ALICIA: Now ... yes. Now I feel ready ... I can do it. *(Like a presentiment.)* It's like a strange force is pushing me over the edge to the other world—a death-like energy inside me but from somewhere else.... *(Forcefully.)* One, two and—

GASPAR: *(Interrupts violently, as if sprung from the earth.)* Just a minute! Don't do it! Not yet!

ALICIA: *(Terrified.)* Who are you? Where did you come from? *(Furious.)* Go away! Now! Go on, leave me alone! Don't you realize that this moment belongs to me?

GASPAR: *(Trying to placate her.)* Miss, please believe me. It's not my intention to stop you or to dissuade you from your decision. On the contrary ...

ALICIA: Get out of here! *(Discovers a mini tape-recorder on GASPAR. Panicked.)* Why are you carrying a tape-recorder?

GASPAR: You're carrying a weapon and I haven't asked *you* why.

ALICIA: *(Furious.)* A tape-recorder can also be a weapon.

GASPAR: Possibly ... but not in my hands. *(Sincerely.)* I am a good man. I earn an honest living.

ALICIA: *(Trying to calm herself down and to believe him at the same time.)* If you're really a good man, please have consideration and respect for me.

GASPAR: Of course. Just tell me what you need.

ALICIA: *(With complete certainty.)* I need to be alone.

Scene Five

(MUSIC: Suspense music, with chords that finalize ALICIA's last sentence.)

MC: Well dear listeners, we're at a crucial moment. *(Trying with each question to create emotional tension in the audience.)* Will Gaspar succeed in his mission? Will he be able to offer us this direct and so-very-human testimony?

(MUSIC: "That's Extraordinary!" theme.)

(In a hard-sell, advertising tone.) You are listening to "That's Extraordinary!" The most successful radio program on the international airwaves.

(MUSIC: Catchy, upbeat "You have just won..." tune.)

And why are we successful? Because we stop at nothing to bring to your ears, raw and untreated, reality itself! At whatever the cost!

(MUSIC: Smooth, romantic melody.)

(Suggestively.) Alicia needs to be alone. *(Ironically.)* She doesn't know that thousands of people are following her every move.

(MUSIC: Suspense music returns.)

Scene Six

ALICIA: *(Fed up.)* Didn't you say you would leave me alone?

GASPAR: *(In a penetrating, sympathetic tone.)* You are going to be alone forever. *Really* alone. What's your hurry? Let me offer you my company... as a friend.

ALICIA: There's no time left for that.

GASPAR: *(Wounded.)* But I need you to help me.

ALICIA: *(Beside herself.)* You want *me* to help *you*? Why don't you go and ask someone more...

GASPAR: *(Feelingly.)* More... what?

ALICIA: More able to help you.

GASPAR: I need *your* help, Alicia.

ALICIA: *(Shocked.)* How do you know my name? Who told you my name is Alicia?

GASPAR: *(Seductively.)* When someone attracts me, really attracts me I mean, her name suddenly appears to me out of nowhere, as clear and bright as day. From the moment I saw you, I knew your name. I saw you ... so distant, so beautiful, lost in the middle of this wood, at the very cliff edge of your own life, and I said to myself: Her name is Alicia.

ALICIA: *(Falling for the flattery for an instant.)* Really? Nothing like this has ever happened to me before.

GASPAR: *(Leading her.)* Nothing like ... what?

ALICIA: *(Moved.)* Nothing—magic. That someone could guess my name ...

GASPAR: *(Taking advantage of the weak flank she has offered him.)* It's not only your name that I can guess, Alicia....

ALICIA: *(Surprised.)* What more can you guess?

GASPAR: *(In a carefully controlled, calculated voice.)* Your deepest needs.

ALICIA: I don't need anything anymore.

GASPAR: I'm sorry to contradict you, but it seems so very clear to me that you do need something more, that you're asking for something, that you're even ... crying out for something ...

ALICIA: *(Shocked.)* Me? Asking for something? For what?

GASPAR: *(Attempting to touch her in order to get the interview.)* Love. Love, Alicia. Love. You are asking me for love.

Scene Seven

(MUSIC: Romantic, something worn out and in bad taste; continues underneath.)

MC: *(Enthusiastic.)* Yes! Oh yes! Now our own reporter Gaspar Wolf is really showing us how to reach the human soul. *(Demagogic.)* I have tears in my eyes, and if my voice breaks ... *(His voice breaks.)* it's because *(With difficulty, as if about to cry.)* I'm thinking of her, of Alicia. I can picture her enormous aquatic eyes mooring themselves in the penetrating gaze of Gaspar Wolf. His will be the last pair of eyes that she will see—the last pair of eyes that will look at her.

(MUSIC: Ends.)

Scene Eight

ALICIA: Why are you talking to me about love, now? I've looked for love all my life. Now I need to be alone, by myself.

GASPAR: *(Almost in secret.)* Love cures all ills.

ALICIA: It's late ... too late ...

GASPAR: Give me a chance. *(Insistent.)* Give yourself a chance.

ALICIA: A chance for what?

GASPAR: I want to do ... an interview with you ... before ... before ... you abandon us forever.

ALICIA: *(Bewildered.)* An interview? With me? And who's going to be interested in this interview?

GASPAR: Lots of people, Alicia.

ALICIA: I don't understand ...

GASPAR: You ... could tell the world ... what it feels like before you die. And since all of us are going to die sooner or later ... who wouldn't be interested?

ALICIA: But what good is it to me to do an interview that won't come out until after I'm dead?

GASPAR: It will be for the good of humanity.

ALICIA: I have already said goodbye to humanity.

GASPAR: And above all it will be for the good of my family.

ALICIA: Your family?

GASPAR: *(Pathetic.)* An interview like this could help us ... financially.

ALICIA: I don't understand.

GASPAR: Excuse my ... presumption, but you are in a position to do something really—an interview with someone who's about to take her own life—it's very original.... They would pay me very well for it, and that would help my family to get out of the financial mess that we're in. It would mean my children could eat ...

ALICIA: Your children are hungry?

GASPAR: *(Nervously.)* Well, you see, I don't have any work right now. Well—actually—to be honest, it's been quite a while since I've had any work, since I've sold even a word.

Scene Nine

(MUSIC: "That's Extraordinary!" theme.)

MC: Extraordinary strategy of our reporter, Gaspar Wolf! He's demonstrating to us the techniques of the shrewd and clever journalist, the modern journalist without prejudice or fear.... Will he pull off this final interview with Alicia by pretending to be a poor, unemployed father?

(MUSIC: Suspenseful; building.)

Stay tuned to "That's Extraordinary!" The program that investigates humanity in the service of humanity!

(MUSIC: Theme music.)

Scene Ten

GASPAR: Well, now I've confessed to you *my* tragedy. *(Snivelling.)* Only you can help me, Alicia. But it's true you have no reason to help me. You have already broken free from the chains of reality. Why should you bother about me? You have every right to throw me out, to insult me ... *(Pitifully.)* You could damn me to hell, Alicia, and I would understand perfectly.

ALICIA: Look, I—

GASPAR: *(False tears.)* Yes?

ALICIA: I ... never ...

GASPAR: Do you want me to leave right now?

ALICIA: *(Confused, anxious.)* Don't cry. Please don't cry, sir.

GASPAR: *(Cries.)* It's nothing. It'll pass. Excuse my insolence. I'm going now.

ALICIA: I ... look, don't go ... I can do it ... in a few minutes. I'll do the interview. At least my death will feed your children.

Scene Eleven

(MUSIC: Happy, triumphant.)

MC: *(As if GASPAR has scored a goal.)* He scores! He scores! Our own Gaspar Wolf has broken through the defences of the unassailable Alicia, yes he has! Wonderful effectiveness in the approach, gentlemen, don't you think? This great offensive move on the part of our man means that we can now present to you a world première. Yes, for the first time anywhere in the world, ladies and gentlemen, an interview with a suicide a mere instant before her departure to the other world.

(MUSIC: Sports march.)

Alicia leaves this world, valiant and resolute. And we will respect her unquestionable will. All we want is to be secret witnesses to her final confessions.

(MUSIC: Nostalgic, "We'll meet again"; continues underneath.)

Alicia is not alone. Our white handkerchiefs are fluttering in the wind in gestures of: Farewell.

(SOUND/MUSIC: "Farewell" echoes and fades; harps, in bad taste.)

We are like secret spies on her private journey of no return. Silent, hidden behind our radios large or small, you and I are the privileged witnesses to the unfolding of this final tragedy, while she, of course, is completely unaware of our presence.

(MUSIC: More intense, sentimental, nostalgic; continues underneath.)

She is an unknown, an anonymous being from the anonymous city. But we have come to say goodbye. And although she doesn't know it, we have come to accompany her.

(MUSIC: Well-known children's tune; continues underneath.)

Alicia too was once a little girl.... She too frolicked in the park with her little friends, surely unaware of what life had prepared for her.

(MUSIC: Children singing a well-known tune.)

(Exploitingly.) An innocent little girl who pranced about among the poppies, the same poppies that today bid her farewell.

(MUSIC: Sudden loud rock music; continues underneath.)

And then Alicia became an adolescent. An adolescent who danced, happy and carefree, just like you ... or me, to the beat of rock and roll.

(MUSIC: Romantic Bolero music; continues underneath.)

Until one day Alicia, also just like you or me, found love. The first love. The first kiss. *(Hums along with the music.)* And perhaps it was then that she also came to know her first pain....

(SOUND: Radio sound effect, intense rain; continues underneath.)

Surely it was raining. And Alicia was walking in that rain, without her umbrella, thinking of him.

(MUSIC: "Singing in the Rain.")

Then, one day, a day like any other day, it stopped raining. And Alicia, hardly realizing, began to laugh.

(SOUND: Radio sound effect, youthful, fun-loving laughter.)

Whatever became of that youthful laughter? Who shattered it?

(SOUND: Radio sound effect, broken glass.)

Who was it that suddenly slammed the door?

(SOUND: Radio sound effect, violent door slam.)

Who was it that left her yet again in absolute and devastating solitude?

(SOUND: Radio sound effect, car starts, accelerates, screeches away.)

Who? When? How was she brought to this final ending?

(MUSIC: "That's Extraordinary!" theme.)

But enough of fantasies. Let's listen to the real Alicia.

(MUSIC: Soft music.)

Let's hear what she herself has to say....

Scene Twelve

(SOUND: Birds singing in the trees.)

ALICIA: Well, what would you like to know, sir?

GASPAR: I was just listening to the birds singing and it seemed to me that their song was dedicated to you.

(SOUND: Singing and chattering of birds intensifies.)

ALICIA: It's true. They're marvellous ... with their feathers of all colours and their brilliant beaks ... the way they fly. Look at that one perched on the top branch.

(SOUND: Happy cheeping of one bird.)

If only I could perch on the highest branch and take to the air, flying towards the immense sky ...

GASPAR: Have you ever tried?

ALICIA: Yes, I have tried.

(SOUND: Chattering of birds.)

I have tried but I didn't get very far. And whenever I stopped to sing on the branches, usually I could only come out with a sort of "twip, twip," an insipid sound, not very joyful—or graceful for that matter. And most of the time the branch I was sitting on would break anyway, and I'd come crashing down to the ground.

(SOUND: Singing of birds intensifies.)

They sing as if life were worth living.... They sing innocently because they don't know anything about loneliness.

(SOUND: One bird sings alone, marvellously.)

Can you hear that? That one sings better than the rest. He's a real virtuoso. *(Whistles to the bird, hoping for an answer.)*

(SOUND: The bird answers, imitating ALICIA exactly.)

He heard me! He's answering me! *(Whistles again, this time a more complicated melody.)*

(SOUND: The bird repeats the new tune.)

GASPAR: He heard you! He is answering you!

ALICIA: Yes! I've made a friend! *(To the bird.)* Let's see if you can do this tune. *(Whistles with more variations.)*

(SOUND: The bird replies with exactly the same tune.)

Oh! This is really incredible! What have I done all my life that I never paid any attention to the birds? Why did I have to come to this extreme before I could even notice how beautiful, how generous nature is?

(SOUND: Now the bird suggests a tune.)

He's talking to me. Excuse me. I should reply. *(Whistles what the bird has just whistled.)*

(SOUND: The bird speaks to her intently and at length.)

Oh! I think I understand what the bird is saying to me.

GASPAR: *(Impatient.)* You and I were going to have a little conversation.

ALICIA: I'm sorry, it's just that at the last minute I'm discovering things I never dreamed of. I've been deaf, dumb and blind all my life. I'm just beginning to realize how lazy I've been, how I've—

GASPAR: Do we do this interview?

ALICIA: Wouldn't it be better to listen to the birds?

(SOUND: A real uproar from all the birds, a riot of happy singing.)

GASPAR: *(Fed up.)* I didn't come here to listen to the birds sing, Miss.

ALICIA: I didn't either. But suddenly—

GASPAR: Let's just leave the little birdies aside ...

ALICIA: Why?

GASPAR: What do you mean, why? You haven't come to this crucial point in your life just to amuse yourself with the singing of little birds. You came here to commit suicide. To commit suicide! Or have you forgotten?

ALICIA: I don't know ...

GASPAR: What do you mean, you don't know?

ALICIA: Maybe I came here to discover the song of the birds.

GASPAR: That's not possible.

ALICIA: Everything's possible. *(Whistles to the birds.)*

(SOUND: The birds answer her.)

Do you hear them? They're talking to me. And do you know what they're saying?

GASPAR: They're saying that every person has an obligation to fulfil her destiny.

ALICIA: They're saying that life is worth the trouble ...

(SOUND: Uproar of birds.)

GASPAR: You're not seeing things clearly.

ALICIA: They're telling me to try again, not to be a coward, to wake up and live. Can you hear them? They're saying that life is always a risk ... that to run away from this world is cowardice. That's what those birds are telling me.

(SOUND: Chattering of birds.)

GASPAR: *(Losing control.)* Enough of the stupid birds! Shut up! They're driving me crazy! I hate them!!

Scene Thirteen

(MUSIC: "That's Extraordinary!" theme.)

MC: *(Covering his anxiety.)* It's all going according to plan, ladies and gentlemen. Our beloved Alicia has been deeply moved by the sweet singing of the birds, and this can only mean that in a little while she too will take to the air and fly, fly just like one of those little birds ...

(MUSIC: Nostalgic.)

One more bird among the thousands of birds that cross the night in glorious flight. She will fly ... she will fly so high ... and perhaps she will even reach the very source of light. Perhaps, from way up there, she will be able to see all of us, strolling through life ... and perhaps she will even send us a sign so that we can recognize her.

(MUSIC: Vivaldi's "Gloria"; continues underneath.)

She is ready to begin her flight. Her delicate wings have already begun to flutter. She is preparing herself for that eternal ascension ...

Scene Fourteen

ALICIA: You seem bothered, sir. What's the matter? It's not the birds, is it?

GASPAR: *(Trying to control his rage.)* I was alone with you. Nobody was listening to us. It was like we were in our own glass bubble. And suddenly the place fills up with birds, talking birds, birds that talk to you. Look. You and I know that birds don't talk. You and I know that they chirp and that you are only hearing what you would like to hear.

ALICIA: Don't tell me you're jealous!

GASPAR: *(Romantic.)* Very jealous.

ALICIA: *(Laughs.)* Jealous of the birds?

GASPAR: Jealous of the birds.

ALICIA: They are asking me to live. And you?

GASPAR: I am not a bird.

ALICIA: Yes, I know that.

GASPAR: I am asking you to talk to me before you die.

ALICIA: To talk ...

GASPAR: Yes, Alicia. I am asking you to talk to me in private before being silenced forever.

ALICIA: Of course. I understand. You want to appropriate my final words, isn't that right?

GASPAR: *(Implacable.)* Good. I see you do understand. Speak to me, Alicia ...

ALICIA: What do you want me to talk about? *(Lucid and ferocious.)* You want me to entertain you with my romantic failures? Fine. The man I loved left me for my best friend. And now do you want to know about my personal frustrations? I wanted to be a dancer and I'm nothing. Do you know the taste, the smell of Nothing? Anything else? I have an alcoholic father who used to beat up my mother—who's paralysed. Is that the kind of news that sells?

GASPAR: Now we're on the right track, Alicia. It's the track of human beings, not birds, dear. So. Your father used to beat your mother?

ALICIA: And not only my mother, but my brothers and sisters too, and me. Are you taping? Is this what you want from me?

GASPAR: Yes, yes. I'm taping. Go on.

ALICIA: What else do you want to know?

GASPAR: Why did you come to this extreme, wanting to take your own life?

ALICIA: Because I didn't have birds around me....

(SOUND: Cheering of birds.)

GASPAR: That's nonsense!

ALICIA: And because I was alone and confused ... confused like I am now when I look at you.

GASPAR: I'm not confusing you.

ALICIA: You could tell me the same thing that the birds are telling me.... Now ... right now ... if ...

GASPAR: Alicia, we are human beings.

ALICIA: *(Desperate.)* Say something.... Please. Don't leave me alone!

GASPAR: Fine. I say goodbye and good luck.

ALICIA: *(Very anxious.)* That's all?

GASPAR: Now it's your turn to say goodbye.

ALICIA: Will a shot in the head sell? Is that what you're longing for?

GASPAR: *(Panicked.)* Look, there's no need to point that gun at me.

ALICIA: *(Decided.)* Now you answer me. The reason you don't want to help me to live is because you don't want to lose this interview. It's business, isn't it?

GASPAR: Put the gun down. We are civilized people. I didn't come here to die. I came here to—

ALICIA: To see me die! You want me to put the gun to my head, am I right? *(Sudden.)* Who sent you? Who do you work for? Answer me or I'll kill you!

GASPAR: It's not my fault! It wasn't my idea! I work for the radio program "That's Extraordinary!" It's the truth, I swear.

ALICIA: "That's Extraordinary!"? You mean thousands of people are listening to this!? You mean that all that stuff about the humble, unemployed journalist was a lie?

(SOUND: A shot.)

GASPAR: My God! Help! She wants to kill me!

(SOUND: Two shots.)

ALICIA: Run away! Run away, coward!

(SOUND: One shot.)

Coward! You can't even stand up to me. You want to sell my death for a good price! Well, I'm not going to give you the pleasure! I'm going to follow the birds' advice.

(SOUND: Happy cheering from the birds.)

I'm going to take a gamble on life ...

(SOUND: Cheering of birds.)

Alicia is going to dare to start over again! Attention, audience of "That's Extraordinary!", wherever you are ... *(To herself.)* I suppose there are microphones hidden around here somewhere....

(SOUND: Rustling of leaves, bushes.)

No one's going to make a circus out of my death! Do you hear? I'm throwing away this gun! I'm going to live! I'm sorry to have to disappoint the morbid, bloodthirsty audience....

(SOUND: Rustling of bushes, very close on.)

I know my life is no good for business, for this sinister program directed by—

GASPAR: *(Secretly, whispering.)* Hello, sound? Cut. Sound, cut. Cut the—

ALICIA: Aha! There it is! Give me that microphone! Give it to me! Attention, all of you in the audience of—

GASPAR: Sound—cut cut cut!! Hey—

(SOUND: Grunts, rustling, etc. A scuffle, very close on, over the microphone; continues underneath.)

GASPAR: Don't you—give me that mike right now. Give me that!!

ALICIA: No I won't!!

(SOUND: Scuffling.)

Scene Fifteen

(SOUND: Radio interference, static.)

MC: There seems to be ... uh ... some interference on the line, ladies and gentlemen. Regrettably we are forced to interrupt our transmission.

(MUSIC/SOUND: Static. "That's Extraordinary!" theme, sped up. Chattering of birds as on location. Sound is picked up again. Static, then:)

GASPAR: *(Struggling.)* Would you give that to me? It's not yours, it's mine.

ALICIA: I want to talk to the audience. I want to tell them—

GASPAR: Shut up! Just shut up! Cut the sound! Cut cut cut cut cut—

(MUSIC/SOUND: Theme music, a few bars, static.)

ALICIA: I'm alive! You can't gag me! I'm alive!

(SOUND: They scuffle, close on over mike.)

Give me that earphone! I want to hear what they're saying!

(MUSIC: Theme established.)

MC: And so, ladies and gentlemen, we have saved a life today! And is this not perhaps the mission of a humanitarian program such as our own?

(SOUND: Static.)

ALICIA: Criminals! Liars!

(SOUND: Static.)

GASPAR: Cut cut cut!

(SOUND: Static.)

MC: We're not actually hearing Alicia very well just now, but we know that she's grateful. We have a few technical problems, uh ... as I mentioned before there seems to be some kind of interference in our transmission. But doubtless if she could Alicia would want to say thank you to us all.

(MUSIC: Triumphal march.)

This has certainly been an unforeseen conclusion to our program today.... Marvellous! Alicia, grateful, deeply moved, is perhaps even now on her knees blessing "That's Extraordinary!" for saving her life.... And I must say it is wonderful to be able to do some good in this world, even from our own modest and humble program, "That's Extraordinary!"—the hottest radio program on the international airwaves! Until next week, friends!

(MUSIC: That's Extraordinary! theme.)

Also available from Blizzard Publishing

The Morningside Dramas
TAKE FIVE
EDITED BY DAVE CARLEY

Every morning hundreds of thousands of Canadians tune into CBC Radio's flagship program, Morningside. It's a fine and noble addiction, fed in parts by host Peter Gzowski's intelligent interviews and the program's belief that no story is too great or small to tackle, no corner of the country too obscure to illuminate. The final offering of every Morningside morning—the aural dessert—is the radio play, an eclectic and sometimes controversial presentation of comedy and drama.

Take Five brings to print five of the best dramas from the 1990-91 season. The tall tales of **Richardo Keens-Douglas'** native Grenada come to vibrant life in his *Once upon an Island*. **Timothy Findley** has adapted three stories by Anton Chekhov, all dealing with fidelity gone drastically awry, in *Love and Deception*. **Arthur Milner's** dry and witty *The City* examines the crashing ideals and practical considerations of the thirty-something set in their renovated big-city ghettos. *The Skid*, by **Thomas Lackey**, displays the full potential of radio for evoking just about any environment and event—even the creation of the world! Finally, **Mary Burns** has adapted her own tough and controversial stories on northern life in *Yukon Quintette*.

Dave Carley (editor) is the author of the popular and widely produced plays *Midnight Madness* and *Writing with our Feet*. Prior to his current position as script editor of the Morningside radio dramas, Mr. Carley was at the Playwrights Union of Canada as editor of that organization's playscripts and journal *CanPlay*.

$14.95 (pb) ISBN 0-921368-21-6